TSO/E CLIST:
The Complete Tutorial
and Desk Reference

Books from QED

Database

Building the Data Warehouse
Migrating to DB2
DB2: The Complete Guide to Implementation
  and Use
DB2 Design Review Guidelines
DB2: Maximizing Performance of Online
  Production Systems
Embedded SQL for DB2
SQL for DB2 and SQL/DS Application
  Developers
Using DB2 to Build Decision Support Systems
Logical Data Base Design
Entity-Relationship Approach to Logical
  Database Design
Database Management Systems
Database Machines and Decision Support
  Systems
IMS Design and Implementation Techniques
Repository Manager/MVS
How to Use ORACLE SQL*PLUS
ORACLE: Building High Performance Online
  Systems
ORACLE Design Review Guidelines
Using ORACLE to Build Decision Support
  Systems
Understanding Data Pattern Processing
Developing Client/Server Applications in an
  Architected Environment

Systems Engineering

Information Systems Architecture in the 90's
Quality Assurance for Information Systems
The User-Interface Screen Design Handbook
Managing Software Projects
The Complete Guide to Software Testing
A User's Guide for Defining Software
  Requirements
A Structured Approach to Systems Testing
Rapid Application Prototyping: A New
  Approach to User Requirements Analysis
The Software Factory
Data Architecture
Advanced Topics in Information Engineering
Software Engineering with Formal Metrics

Management

Introduction to Data Security and Controls
How to Automate Your Computer Center:
  Achieving Unattended Operations

Management (cont'd)

Controlling the Future
The UNIX Industry Ethical Conflicts in
  Information and Computer Science,
  Technology, and Business
Mind Your Business

Data Communications

Designing and Implementing Ethernet Networks
Network Concepts and Architectures
Open Systems

IBM Mainframe Series

CICS/VS: A Guide to Application Debugging
CICS Application and System Programming:
  Tools and Techniques
CICS: A Guide To Performance Tuning
MVS COBOL II Power Programmer's Desk
  Reference
VSE JCL and Subroutines for Application
  Programmers
VSE COBOL II Power Programmer's Desk
  Reference
The MVS Primer
TSO/E CLISTs: The Complete Tutorial and
  Desk Reference
QMF: How to Use Query Management Facility
  with DB2 and SQL/DS
DOS/VSE: Introduction to the Operating
  System
DOS/VSE JCL: Mastering Job Control
  Language
DOS/VSE: CICS Systems Programming
DOS/VSE/SP Guide for Systems Programming
Advanced VSE System Programming
  Techniques
Systems Programmer's Problem Solver
VSAM: Guide to Optimization and Design
MVS/JCL: Mastering Job Control Language
MVS/TSO: Mastering CLISTs
MVS/TSO: Mastering Native Mode and ISPF
REXX in the TSO Environment

Programming

C Language for Programmers
VAX/VMS: Mastering DCL Commands and
  Utilities
The PC Data Handbook
UNIX C Shell Desk Reference

QED books are available at special quantity discounts for educational uses, premiums, and sales promotions. Special books, book excerpts, and instructive materials can be created to meet specific needs.

This is Only a Partial Listing. For Additional Information or a Free Catalog contact
QED Information Sciences, Inc. • P. O. Box 82-181 • Wellesley, MA 02181
Telephone: 800-343-4848 or 617-237-5656 or fax 617-235-0826

TSO/E CLIST:
The Complete Tutorial
and Desk Reference

Charles H. Rider

QED Technical Publishing Group
Boston • Toronto • London

© 1992 QED Information Sciences, Inc.
P.O. Box 82-181
Wellesley, MA 02181

QED Technical Publishing Group is a division of QED Information Sciences, Inc.

Library of Congress Catalog Number: 91-43964
International Standard Book Number: 0-89435-407-8

Printed in the United States of America

92 93 94   10 9 8 7 6 5 4 3 2 1

Library of Congress Cataloging-in-Publication Data

Rider, Charles H.
    TSO CLIST : the complete tutorial and desk reference / Charles H. Rider.
        p.   cm.
    Includes index.
    ISBN 0-89435-407-8
    1. Time-sharing computer systems.   2. CLIST (Computer program language)   I. Title.
    QA76.53.R54   1992
    005.4'42—dc20   91-43964
                                                              CIP

*For my wife
Sharron*

Contents

Preface

A CLIST is the command procedure language in the IBM MVS TSO interactive environment. CLIST means simply "command list." This feature of the IBM interactive capability enables users to maintain TSO commands in a dataset and to execute those TSO commands with the additional functions provided by the CLIST language. Hence the term "command procedures."

The IBM command procedure language is rich in capabilities, flexibility and a variety of features. Development of a command procedure is simple when the few simple rules are followed. This book will assist you in developing and using command procedures.

This book has several important objectives. First, it is an excellent primer in the CLIST language and is designed as an aid in teaching the new student this language. This book not only presents all of the syntax and rules for the proper coding of the language elements, it provides all of the more important statements, operands, operators and elements that are necessary to develop reliable and effective procedures. But, perhaps more importantly, this book also emphasizes the underlying concepts of the language. By exploring the basic fundamentals of CLISTs, an understanding of "why" is thereby facilitated. This not only assists in development of better command procedures, it makes them more interesting and fun.

Second, it will serve as a ready reference manual as you are developing and testing command procedures. All of the CLIST statements and their operands and all of the system variables and built-in functions are presented in a concise format and organized into topics titled with the name of that statement or variable. Moreover, these topics include extensive notes to clarify the material. Usually, these notes will resolve many of the problems that may occur.

Third, this book is designed to clarify and amplify material provided by vendors such as IBM by emphasizing the advantages and disadvantages of command procedure statements and variables, and by detailing ways to avoid inefficiencies and problems.

Fourth, the major objective of this book is to encourage you to use the command procedure language in a most advantageous and productive manner, to use all the features of this very powerful language, and to be comfortable in using CLISTs.

TSO/E CLIST: The Complete Tutorial and Desk Reference is logically arranged into eleven chapters.

Chapter 1 discusses the basic concepts of command procedures and their purposes. It also presents an introduction to the functional features of this powerful language.

Chapter 2 presents many of the pitfalls that can occur when command procedures are not used properly. It offers several guidelines to improve the efficiency of developing and using a command procedure.

Chapter 3 gives in great detail the proper structure and syntax required to code the statements, variables and expressions of the language.

Chapter 4 discusses the creation of online disk datasets to serve as libraries for CLIST procedures. It also emphasizes how procedures can be easily and reliably tested before they are placed into production or given to end users.

Chapter 5 offers an extensive and detailed discussion of how command procedures are executed in the interactive and batch environments.

Chapter 6 introduces the concept of processing flow when the CLIST is executed. Statement execution is usually in serial order, but several CLIST operations can alter the sequence of operations. Chapter 6 discusses branches to other points in the CLIST, execution of DO groups, user interrupts and error conditions, and executing nested CLISTs and subprocedures.

Chapters 7, 8 and 9 discuss, in detail, the syntax and usage of all components of the language. These chapters offer, by discussion and by example, a thorough review of all elements of the CLIST language.

Each of the arithmetic, logical and comparison operations of the CLIST language and their usage is provided in Chapter 7.

Chapter 8 covers the use of variables in command procedures. It discusses the several types of variables and how they are used for initiation parameters, for input/output operations, and to transfer values to nested CLISTs or to subprocedures. Chapter 8 also discusses user variables and global variables as well as the 61 system-defined variables and the 11 system built-in functions.

In Chapter 9, each of the 32 CLIST statements is examined in depth. These statements are classified into nine categories based on their operational function. The discussion of each of the 32 statements is provided in a simple format designed to facilitate readability and future reference. This format fully describes the function of the statement, the syntax of the statement, all of the statement's operands, and examples of the use of the statement. Explanatory notes are given to clarify the information and to emphasize critical points.

Chapter 10 gives examples of actual command procedures that have been used in a real production environment.

Finally, Chapter 11 lists the IBM codes issued when an error condition occurs.

Some of the chapters include exercises to illustrate the use and capabilities of the many elements of the CLIST language. These exercises will enhance your understanding of the CLIST statements and operations. Solutions for all exercises have been provided in the Appendix at the end of this book.

Introduction

A CLIST is an online file containing statements that can be executed in TSO. The CLIST may consist of one or any number of TSO commands and CLIST statements in any combination and, when the CLIST is executed, the commands and statements will be performed. The CLIST may also contain any number of user- or system-defined variables. It will also perform logical, arithmetic, comparison and branching operations. Therefore, a CLIST is similar to a program or command procedure.

There are many useful purposes for CLISTs. They are usually written and executed to perform the following:

- Simple execution of multiple operations
- Conditional execution of operations
- Repetitive execution of the same operations
- Execution with parameters and variables
- Interaction with end users
- Simple arithmetic and logical operations
- Error and interrupt detection

There are many functional features available in CLISTs. The functions may be categorized as command execution; variables and functions; input and output operations; and comments and notation.

Command execution refers to the invoking or operation of the CLIST. The CLIST is executed under TSO by the command EXEC; EXEC may specify optional parameters. Multiple commands and subcommands contained in the CLIST will be executed with the single TSO command EXEC. This is valuable in performing any set of multiple commands and operations repetitively without having to re-enter the statements each time. A procedure is therefore retained for re-execution at any time. Moreover, the procedure may include variables as execution parameters so that values passed to the procedure may be different each time the CLIST is executed.

Basic control options may be in effect during execution of all or selected operations in the CLIST. As an example, the statements in the CLIST can be displayed at the terminal as they are executed; this feature can be turned on and off at any point in the CLIST.

Additional command execution features include the capability to assign labels to statements so that they may be an object for a branching or return operation. Statement execution and branching may be dependent upon the results of a condition test. The execution of the CLIST procedure or of any of its statements may be performed based on the detection of errors and interrupts.

Programs, other routines and nested CLISTs may be called and executed within the CLIST. Variables and parameters may be passed to or received from the called programs, routines and nested CLISTs.

Variables and functions are those functional features of the CLIST language that enable the user to specify user-defined variables or to access system-defined variables. Variables can be defined and set, or can be reset with new values, at any point in the CLIST procedure. System variables are used to obtain information about the CLIST, the user and the host environment. Some of the system variables can be set by the user, while others cannot.

Built-in CLIST functions enable the user to perform logical evaluations. This capability allows the user to compute the value of an arithmetic expression, to determine that a value is character or numeric, to determine the length of either a character string or numeric expression, to specify that the variable is to be treated only as a character string, and to specify a substring or a range of consecutive characters in a variable.

Built-in functions also enable the computation of arithmetic expressions. Fixed-point arithmetic can be performed on any numeric values and/or expressions.

Input/output operations are the functional feature of CLISTs that enable reading information from an online file or from a user's terminal as well as writing data to an online file or to a user's terminal. Input/output operations for online files consist of reading or writing records in the file. An online file can be opened for input, output or both. Input/output operations to a user's terminal accept input data the user enters at the terminal or displays information produced by the CLIST procedure.

The functional feature that allows comments and notation in the CLIST provides for full self-documentation. Comments and notation can be encoded anywhere after the first statement. They can be written as separate statements or included on an executable statement.

Efficient Command Procedures

CLIST procedures are an effective and efficient method for storing and performing repetitive, multiple TSO commands and operating processes. However, there are certain conditions for which a CLIST is not recommended. A CLIST procedure can be inefficient for some operations. In addition, CLISTs may be difficult to write and test for some kinds of operations.

First, it is important to note that CLISTs are not compiled. Upon CLIST initiation, every statement in the procedure will be scanned for syntax errors. If any errors are discovered, execution of the CLIST will not start. Furthermore, during execution, the syntax of each statement is checked before it is performed. Examination of the statement occurs each time the statement is executed. This is necessary because values in variables and other conditions are subject to change.

Therefore, because the CLIST is not compiled like a program, it is interpreted when it is started, and each statement will be checked every time it is executed. This is not efficient if the CLIST consists of many statements or complex routines requiring extensive substitution and evaluation.

CLISTs should not be used for long sequences of operations. The procedure that contains many hundreds of statements may be a better candidate for a higher-level language, which will be compiled for execution. This avoids the lengthy, perhaps repetitive, interpretation of statements.

Multiple, complex loops should be avoided since each of the statements must be interpreted for each iteration of a loop. This is particularly true if complex routines to evaluate an expression or perform extensive substitution are embedded in the loop.

Highly complex mathematical expressions should be avoided because they can be difficult to encode and test. These expressions most often contain multiple variables. Substitution is done every time the variable is used. Moreover, a statement will be scanned multiple times because symbolic substitution for variables is performed in a hierarchical fashion. The first scan of a statement resolves variables at the lowest level. The next scan resolves the next higher level of values. The process is continued until all variables are resolved. This is inefficient for complex expressions executed many times.

Extensive file input or output operations should be avoided. CLIST read/write statements are very inefficient compared to the capabilities of a compiled program. These statements to read or write an online file must first be interpreted. The records are then substituted for the designated variable.

In summary, a CLIST should not be used where the application clearly calls for a program that can be compiled. Specific guidelines cannot be given for a number of CLIST statements, for complexity of expressions and operations, and for a number of records to be read or written. In fact, the decision to use a CLIST or other language depends on the combination of these factors, the frequency of using the CLIST, the ease of coding a CLIST, and many other elements.

3

Statement Structure and Syntax

Each line in a CLIST procedure is a statement. A CLIST may consist of one or any number of statements. All statements must conform to a basic structure, although the format of the statement may be free-form. All CLIST statements must begin with either a CLIST command or a TSO command or subcommand. This is the verb, or "action," part of the statement and tells the system what operation is to be performed. The command or subcommand is usually followed by one or more operands to specify the objects of the operation. Operands may consist of expressions or a dependent command or operand.

3.1   STATEMENT STRUCTURE

The structure of each CLIST statement must be of the form:

WRITENR	ENTER NAME OF MONTH
command	operand

SET	&A = ((4 + &B) / &C)
command	operand

IF	&A = 7	,	THEN	GOTO	LABEL1
command	operand		command	command	operand
					operand

In the first example, the command WRITENR is the verb that instructs the system to write a message to a user's terminal with no carriage return. Thus, the screen cursor remains at the end of the message instead of being placed at the first position of the next line. The operand "ENTER NAME OF MONTH" is the message to be displayed at the user's terminal.

In the second example, SET is the command to set a variable equal to the result of evaluating an expression. The terms prefixed with an ampersand are variables. The operand "&A = ((4 + &B) / &C)" means that 4 is to be added to the value of the variable "B" and the result will be divided by the value in the variable "C". The variable "A" will be set equal to the final result. The values in "B" and "C" do not change.

In the third example, the command IF instructs the system to test the condition stated in the operand "&A = 7". If the condition is true, the dependent operand following THEN will be performed. The object of the THEN command is its operand "GOTO LABEL1". It consists of both a dependent command GOTO and its operand "LABEL1". If the condition is not true, the GOTO command will not be executed.

3.2   DELIMITERS

The CLIST language requires use of one or more delimiters to separate each command and operand in each statement. Either spaces or commas may be used as delimiters. It is suggested that a space serve as the delimiter to improve readability.

At least one delimiter must follow the command before any of the operands. Delimiters must be coded between each operand in the statement. In addition, a delimiter must be included after the closing colon for a label.

Within an expression, delimiters may be used to separate the various terms and variables. They also separate arithmetic, logical and comparison operators from the terms in the CLIST expression, although they may be optional.

However, caution must be used if delimiters are omitted from an expression. For example, delimiters must be coded to set off letter comparison operators such as EQ and LT but they are optional for symbol comparison operators such as = or <. Similarly, they are also required to separate letter logical operators AND and OR although they are optional for the two symbol logical operators && and |. Delimiters are optional for arithmetic operators.

The use of delimiters is presented in the example below. An "m" indicates that a delimiter is mandatory and an "o" notes that a delimiter is optional. Note the use of a comma after the variable &C to improve the readability of the statement.

```
LABEL1:   IF &A = &B OR &A < &C, THEN SET &C EQ &D + &E
          m  m  o  o  m  m  o  o  m      m   m  m  m  o  o
```

The use of delimiters is presented in the discussion on line continuation, expressions, concatenation of variables, CLIST statement syntax and other topics throughout this book.

3.3 PARENTHESES

Parentheses are used in two ways in CLIST statements.

First, they are necessary to enclose values and expressions associated with the 11 system built-in functions, to enclose values and expressions defined for certain system or keyword variables, and to enclose lists of terms defined for certain operands of CLIST and TSO commands.

Parentheses are also used to control the order of operations in arithmetic operations and evaluation of expressions.

The uses for parentheses are discussed throughout this book, especially in the presentations on arithmetic operations and syntax of expressions.

3.4 LABELS

Any CLIST statement, except PROC and comment statements, may be assigned a label. Labels identify the CLIST statement so that it can be the object of a branch command. For example, processing can be unconditionally transferred to the labeled statement by a GOTO statement with the label as its operand.

Labels can also be used for a logical division of statements in the

CLIST. Thus, groups of logically related statements or coding comprising a specific routine can be identified by assigning a label to the first statement in the routine.

The first statement in a subprocedure in the CLIST must be a PROC . . . . . END statement. PROC . . . . . END statements must be labeled. Subprocedures can be executed only by naming their label in the SYSCALL statement to invoke the subprocedure.

If a statement is labeled, the label must be the first term in the statement, as shown in the example below. Labels may consist of 1 to 31 characters but the first character must be alphabetic. The label must end with a colon (:) and must be followed by at least one delimiter (space or comma).

The following is the correct format for a labeled statement.

```
LABEL1:        SET       &A = &B + &C
 label        command       operand
```

A label must be followed by an executable statement so that no line in a CLIST may consist of only a label. However, it may be continued onto the next line as shown below.

```
LABEL1: +
        SET &A = &B + &C
```

3.5   LINE CONTINUATION

Statements in a CLIST may be continued onto the next line by coding a plus (+) or a minus (−) sign at the end of the line to be continued. A statement may be continued onto multiple lines. However, if the statement is so long that more than one continuation line is required, it may be too complex and the user ought to consider if the operation can be separated into multiple, simple operations.

When a plus sign is used to indicate line continuation, the leading delimiters (spaces and commas) on the next line will be ignored. If a minus sign is used, delimiters on the next line will be retained as a part of the statement.

The delimiters after the last character in the statement and before the continuation character are always retained in the statement. Therefore, all spaces and/or commas preceding a continuation character are considered part of the statement.

The following are examples of line continuation.

The statement

```
IF &A = &B, THEN +
    GOTO LABEL1
```

is interpreted correctly as

```
IF &A = &B, THEN GOTO LABEL1
```

but the statement

```
IF &A = &B, THEN+
    GOTO LABEL1
```

is interpreted incorrectly as

```
IF &A = &B, THENGOTO LABEL1
```

In both examples, the leading spaces in the second line were ignored since a plus sign is used to continue the statement. The three spaces preceding the GOTO command are not treated as delimiters. The first example was interpreted correctly because there is a delimiter (space) preceding the plus sign on the continued line. The second statement was interpreted incorrectly because there is no delimiter after THEN.

The statement

```
WRITE THE CURRENT MONTH -
IS DECEMBER
```

is interpreted correctly as

```
WRITE THE CURRENT MONTH IS DECEMBER
```

but the statement

```
WRITE THE CURRENT MONTH -
      IS DECEMBER
```

is interpreted incorrectly as

```
WRITE THE CURRENT MONTH                    IS DECEMBER
```

In this example, the first entry is correct because there is one space preceding the minus sign. The second entry is not correct because one space preceding the minus sign and seven leading spaces on the second line were retained.

3.6   COMMENTS

Comments can be placed at almost any point in a CLIST. They may be coded as separate statements and as notation on CLIST statements. However, they cannot be the first statement in the CLIST nor can they be included within the text following a WRITE or WRITENR statement or anywhere within a string.

Comments serve as notation for the CLIST and are valuable as self-documentation. It is therefore highly recommended that comments be used liberally. Comments are not interpreted or executed. Therefore, the use of comments has no effect on the performance or efficiency of the CLIST.

Comments may be on the same line as a statement or may be on a separate line. Comments on a statement line could be very useful in documenting the particular statement or any of its expressions or operands. Similarly, comments on one or more separate lines can be valuable in documenting a single CLIST statement or any number of logically related statements.

Comments must be delimited by the use of the slash (/) mark and the asterisk (*). They must be preceded by /* and ended by */. Moreover, comments may be continued onto subsequent lines by the use of the plus (+) and minus (−) signs.

Rules for continuing a comment are the same as for continuing any other CLIST statement. The plus sign causes all leading delimiters to be ignored while the minus sign specifies that all leading delimiters are to be retained for the statement. Of course, since comments are not executed, coding a plus or minus sign is not significant.

The following examples demonstrate the use of comments. The last two entries provide the same notation; they simply demonstrate two different ways to include the comment.

```
GOTO LABEL1          /* Branch to date routine */

/* The next statement is an +
   unconditional branch to date routine */
GOTO LABEL1

/* The next statement is an */
/* unconditional branch to date routine */
GOTO LABEL1
```

It is necessary to note one important caution when comments are used in a CLIST that includes batch JCL statements. JCL is the Job Control Language used for batch processing in the IBM computer system. JCL statements cannot be executed in a CLIST, but they can be encoded using a TSO command such as EDIT and saved or submitted to batch processing. JCL uses a slash and asterisk as the delimiter at the beginning of some JCL statements. They would be read by the CLIST interpreter as comments and will therefore be ignored for processing.

For example, CLIST statements can invoke TSO EDIT to code or modify JCL procedures. These can then be saved or submitted to batch processing. The following example demonstrates the execution of EDIT to create new JCL statements.

```
EDIT MYJCL.CNTL NEW
010 //ABCDE001 JOB .....
020 /*JOBPARM COPIES .....
```

In this example, the "JOBPARM" statement is interpreted as a comment by the CLIST interpreter and is therefore ignored.

One solution to avoid this problem is the following example. Since there is no material coding after the /* in the CHANGE statement, the change to line 020 in the JCL will occur.

```
EDIT MYJCL.CNTL NEW
010 //ABCDE001 JOB .....
020 !!JOBPARM COPIES .....
CHANGE 020 ?!!?/*?
```

3.7   INDENTATION AND PARAGRAPHS

Indenting lines and forming paragraphs in CLISTs, especially when used with labels, spaces and comments, can be extremely valuable for improving readability and understanding of the CLIST. This is valuable during the development and testing of a new CLIST, and it can also be a great advantage in maintaining the CLIST.

This is clearly demonstrated in the following example.

```
LABEL1: SET &B=&B+1
SET &A=&B+&C
IF &A>100 THEN GOTO LABEL2
ELSE GOTO LABEL1
LABEL2: SET &D=&A*&RATE
```

The following is the same code, but the indentation of lines, the addition of spaces between arithmetic operators, and the inclusion of comments significantly enhance its readability.

```
/*                          */
/*    Find amount limit     */
/*                          */
LABEL1: SET &B = &B + 1
        SET &A = &B + &C
        IF &A > 100, THEN GOTO LABEL2
                    ELSE GOTO LABEL1
/*                          */
/*    Calculate maximum value  */
/*                          */
LABEL2: SET &D = &A * &RATE
```

3.8 VARIABLES AND EXPRESSIONS

A symbolic variable is a character string within a CLIST in which an actual value is substituted during execution of the statement. The actual value remains as is unless changed by a subsequent operation. The two kinds of variables are user-defined and system-defined. A user-defined variable is null and has no value until a value is assigned by the user. Some of the system variables also do not have a value until assigned by the system as a result of CLIST execution, while other system variables have values continuously maintained by the system. Many of the system variables may only be read and cannot be modified by the user.

An expression is any combination of variables and operators that are to be evaluated as an arithmetic operation or on which a logical or comparative operation is to be performed. Expressions consist of any number of variables and operators that, when evaluated, produce a result or a condition.

3.8.1 Syntax for Coding Variables

The names of user variables may be 1 to 252 characters. The first character of user variable names must be alphabetic.

The names of system variables and functions are reserved and cannot be used for any other purpose.

Even though a user variable name may be up to 252 characters in length, names from 1 to 8 characters are recommended. The length of variable names in PROC statements cannot exceed 31 characters. Also, variable names used in ISPF panels cannot be greater than 8 characters.

All user and system variable names must be prefixed with one ampersand (&) except when used in the statements in the list below. Conversely, items that begin with a single ampersand are interpreted as a variable name.

Items without an ampersand are not interpreted as variables.

Double ampersands (&&), when preceded and followed by one or more spaces, are processed as the logical operator OR.

The following list presents the CLIST commands for which an ampersand is prohibited or optional. In all other cases, an ampersand is mandatory. It is recommended that an ampersand be used in all cases where it is not expressly prohibited.

PROC statements	—	Prohibited
Dataset I/O statements	—	Prohibited
GLOBAL statements	—	Optional
SET variable =	—	Optional
READ variable	—	Optional
READDVAL variable	—	Optional

A period (.) at the end of a variable name ends the name and separates it from any following characters. A name must end with a period when it is concatenated with another character string that would be interpreted as a part of the name. The following presents several examples of the proper use of the period in a variable name.

```
&MONTH          or    &MONTH.
&MONTH&YEAR     or    &MONTH.&YEAR
&MONTH&YEAR     or    &MONTH.&YEAR.
```

In the examples above, both &MONTH and &YEAR are variables. The CLIST interpreter will recognize each of these variables in each format above because they start with an ampersand.

In the example below, the variable name &MONTH is recognized only in the first entry. In the second entry, the variable name is assumed to be the nine characters MONTH1991.

```
&MONTH.1991     not    &MONTH1991
```

The use of the ending period is particularly critical when a variable name is followed by a character string that begins with a period. This occurs quite often when coding JCL in a CLIST. A period must end the name as shown below.

```
&DSN..DATA      not    &DSN.DATA
```

In this example, if the value of &DSN is assumed to be ABCD, the first entry will be resolved correctly as ABCD.DATA while the second entry is resolved incorrectly as ABCDDATA.

3.8.2   Concatenated Variables

Variable names may be concatenated in a string of any number of variables. Each name must be prefixed with an ampersand. The examples below show three variables concatenated to give a date. Each assumes a value of DECEMBER for &MONTH, 25 for &DAY and 1991 for &YEAR. Both the third and fourth examples below include spaces between the variables.

```
&MONTH&DAY&YEAR        is resolved as   DECEMBER251991
&MONTH.&DAY.&YEAR.     is resolved as   DECEMBER251991
&MONTH &DAY &YEAR      is resolved as   DECEMBER 25 1991
&MONTH. &DAY. &YEAR.   is resolved as   DECEMBER 25 1991
```

3.8.3   Nested Variables

Variables may be included or nested within character strings to create items where only a part is subject to change. The variable names must begin with an ampersand and end with a period. Variables may be coded at the beginning, at the end or anywhere within the character string. The examples below demonstrate the inclusion of variables in character strings. Variable &ABC has a value of ABC; &DEF has a value of DEF.

```
&ABC.XYZ          is resolved as   ABCXYZ
XYZ&ABC           is resolved as   XYZABC
XYZ&ABC.XYZ       is resolved as   XYZABCXYZ
&ABC.&DEF.XYZ     is resolved as   ABCDEFXYZ
XYZ&ABC&DEF.XYZ   is resolved as   XYZABCDEFXYZ
XYZ&ABC.&DEF.XYZ  is resolved as   XYZABCDEFXYZ
```

3.8.4   Expressions

An expression is a string in a CLIST statement that contains one or more variables, character strings, and/or arithmetic, logical and comparative operators. It is to be evaluated as an arithmetic, logical or comparative operation. Because an expression usually contains at least one variable, each of the variables will be resolved and then the operations will be performed. Resolution of a variable means that its value is substituted by replacing its current contents with a user- or system-specified value or with a calculated value.

Arithmetic, logical and/or comparative operators are usually included in an expression. For example, the statement below contains comparative operators (= and <), a logical operator (OR) and an arithmetic operator (+).

```
IF &A = (&B + &C) OR &A < &D, THEN GOTO LABEL1
```

A space preceding and following an operator may be optional or required. The list below indicates the use of spaces for coding operators in an expression. However, it is suggested that spaces always precede and follow an operator to improve readability of the CLIST and to maintain a coding standard.

Letter operators	—	Required
Symbol operators	—	Optional

An expression may be continued onto the next line. However, caution is essential. There is a high potential of error as plus and minus signs are used for both arithmetic operators and line continuation characters. Expressions which include arithmetic operations can be continued only as shown below.

The statement

```
SET &A = &B + &C + &D +
         &E + &F + &G
```

would be interpreted incorrectly as

```
SET &A = &B + &C + &D &E + &F + &G
```

Either of the statements

```
SET &A = &B + &C + &D +      or   SET &A = &B + &C + &D ++
         + &E + &F + &G                    &E + &F + &G
```

would be interpreted correctly as

```
SET &A = &B + &C + &D + &E + &F + &G
```

Expression operations are always executed in priority order. This means that certain types of operations are done before other operations. For example, multiplication is performed before addition. The normal priority of operations follows.

First   –   Positive and negative signs
Second   –   Exponentiation and remainders
Third   –   Multiplication and division
Fourth   –   Addition and subtraction
Fifth   –   Comparison
Sixth   –   Logical AND
Seventh   –   Logical OR

When multiple operators of the highest priority occur on the same statement, those operations are executed right to left, that is, starting from the end of the expression and working to its beginning. For all operations of lower priority, the evaluation proceeds from left to right.

As an example, the following expression will be evaluated in the sequence shown, after all of its variables &B, &C and &D are resolved. The resulting comparison test will be false.

```
IF &A = &B ** 2 + &C / &D - &E
IF 15 =  5 ** 2 + 20 / 10 - 7
IF 15 =      25  + 20 / 10 - 7
IF 15 =      25  +   2    - 7
IF 15 =            20
```

Parentheses are used in arithmetic operations to control the order of operation. They ensure that all operations will be performed in the correct order according to the hierarchical levels specified by the use of parentheses. In the examples below, the resulting values of the arithmetic operations are not the same because of the inclusion of parentheses.

```
SET &A = 2 * 3 + 4          gives &A a value of 10
SET &A = (2 * (3 + 4))      gives &A a value of 14
```

If the example above had included parentheses, the result of the test would be quite different. The condition would then be true as shown below.

```
IF &A = ((&B ** 2) + &C) / (&D - &E)
IF 15 = (( 5 ** 2) + 20) / (10 - 7)
IF 15 = ((    25  ) + 20) / (10 - 7)
IF 15 = ((    25  ) + 20) / (  3   )
IF 15 = ((       45       ) / (  3   )
IF 15 =              15
```

As shown in the above examples, the order of priority may be controlled by using parentheses. Operations are always done on operands in the innermost or lowest level of parentheses first. Then, the next higher level will be performed and so on until all operations are completed.

Parentheses must always be paired. That is, each term that is started with a left parenthesis must be terminated with a right parenthesis. As demonstrated in earlier examples, all terms enclosed in parentheses may contain subordinate terms that are also enclosed in parentheses.

The priority order of operations remains in effect for every term within a pair of parentheses.

3.8.5   Symbolic Substitution

Symbolic substitution is the process of placing a new value in a variable or replacing a current value with a new value. Except for certain variables defined by the system, all user variables and many system variables have no value when first specified and thus cannot be used until set by the user or the system.

Before any CLIST statement can be executed, all variables in the statement must be resolved. This is accomplished by the process known as symbolic substitution.

Substitution occurs from left to right in the statement. If the statement contains nested expressions, that is, terms in parentheses, these variables are resolved first in an inside-to-outside order. Therefore, variables in the lowest level of parentheses are substituted first. The process continues upward through each successive higher level until all of the variables have been resolved.

Symbolic substitution is performed by a process referred to as scanning. As the statement to be executed is evaluated, it is scanned for variables into which real values are to be substituted. Each scan of the statement substitutes values on one level only, starting at the lowest level. The default number of scans per line is 16. This default can be changed by changing the value of the system variable &SYSSCAN to any number from 0 through 2**(31).

The following shows substitution of symbolic variables. The variable &STR indicates that all characters enclosed in the parentheses, that is, the spaces and the comma, are to be treated as an alphanumeric string of characters. The current values of &MONTH, &DAY and &YEAR are DEC, 20 and 1991 respectively. The expression "&DAY.+5" is enclosed in parentheses and will therefore be evaluated first.

Symbolic substitution for the statement

```
SET &DATE = &STR(&MONTH.&STR( )(&DAY.+5)&STR(, )&YEAR.)
```

begins by resolving the lowest level, which is the expression "&DAY.+5":

```
SET &DATE = &STR(&MONTH.&STR( )(20+5)&STR(, )&YEAR.)
SET &DATE = &STR(&MONTH.&STR( )(25)&STR(, )&YEAR.)
```

All remaining variables are on the same level. Substitution proceeds from left to right. First, the variable &MONTH. is assigned the value DEC,

```
SET &DATE = &STR(DEC&STR( )25&STR(, )&YEAR.)
```

a space character is defined for the variable &STR( ),

```
SET &DATE = &STR(DEC 25&STR(, )&YEAR.)
```

a comma and space are defined for the variable &STR(,),

```
SET &DATE = &STR(DEC 25, &YEAR.)
```

and the variable &YEAR. is assigned the value 1991.

```
SET &DATE = &STR(DEC 25, 1991)
```

Last, the variable &STR(DEC 25, 1991) is defined as a string and is therefore treated as alphanumeric characters that are not subject to arithmetic operations.

```
SET &DATE = DEC 25, 1991
```

The actual value of &DATE is now the alphanumeric character string DEC 25, 1991, including the spaces and the comma, which were initially defined by the system variable &STR.

Creating CLISTS

A CLIST resides in a disk dataset that contains one or any number of records. Every record is one line of coding, that is, one statement, although CLIST statements can be continued onto multiple lines or records. These statements may be any CLIST commands, TSO commands and subcommands, and comments.

4.1 CLIST DATASET CHARACTERISTICS

The CLIST file must be online as a disk dataset in order to be executed. It may be a sequential dataset or a member of a partitioned dataset (PDS).

CLIST files must be assigned certain attributes in order for them to be accessible and available for execution. A record format of fixed block (RECFM=FB) is recommended although the record format may be variable (RECFM=VB).

The logical record length should be 80 characters (LRECL=80) for fixed-length records, that is, the dataset has a record format of FB. This is also the IBM standard for the records in JCL (Job Control Language), program source code and other datasets. Other record lengths can be used.

When variable-length records using a record format of VB are specified, the logical record length for the dataset should be 255 characters (LRECL=255).

The table below presents the optimal physical block size for fixed-length records on the disk devices (DASD) installed in most computer facilities. Data is stored on disk volumes in physical blocks of logical records. The physical block size must be an even multiple of the fixed logical record length. Block size is specified by BLKSIZE=nnnn, where "nnnn" is the whole number of bytes in the physical block.

Disk Device	Fixed-Length 80-Character Records		
	Block Size	Records per Block	Records per Track
3390	6480	81	648
3380	6320	79	553
3350	6160	77	231

The block size and therefore the number of records per block and records per track for variable-length records depends on the actual data content of the dataset's records. However, physical block sizes should not exceed 6518 bytes when CLIST datasets reside on 3390 disks, 6356 bytes on 3380 disks and 6233 bytes on 3350 disks.

A user's private CLIST libraries are often concatenated to the system libraries, usually when logging onto the TSO session. Therefore, user dataset attributes should not conflict with those of the system libraries. The best attributes for user CLIST libraries are the attributes of the system libraries.

A CLIST file must be a numbered dataset in order for it to be executable. Line numbers are eight digits and coded into the rightmost eight bytes of each record. In a record with 80 bytes, line numbers are in columns 73 through 80. Lines must be numbered sequentially and in ascending order, but the increments for line numbers may be any value. If a CLIST is not numbered or if its line numbers are not valid, an error condition occurs and the CLIST cannot be executed.

4.2   CLIST DATASET NAMES

The dataset name for a sequential or a partitioned dataset for the CLIST should conform to the standards for IBM naming conventions. Thus, the dataset name should have the suffix CLIST as in the examples below.

```
userid.CLIST

userid.name.CLIST
```

The TSO command EXEC is used to execute a CLIST. It assumes a file type of CLIST if the dataset name is not enclosed in quotes, that is, the name is not fully qualified.

This naming convention enables the user to execute the CLIST by simply issuing its name. For example, if a CLIST file is named 'userid.DATE.CLIST', it can be executed in TSO by the simple command EX DATE. If the dataset type is not CLIST, it can be executed only by the command EXEC followed by its fully qualified name as in EXEC 'userid.DATE.type'.

Similarly, if a CLIST is a member in a partitioned file, the file should be named using the CLIST type. This enables the CLIST to be executed by the file and member names only.

For example, a CLIST named DATE stored in a partitioned dataset named 'userid.ROUTINES.CLIST' can be executed by issuing the command EXEC ROUTINES(DATE). If the partitioned dataset name does not end with CLIST, the CLIST can be executed only by the command EXEC 'userid.ROUTINES.type(DATE)'.

Moreover, a partitioned dataset can be named 'userid.CLIST' and its CLIST members can be executed in TSO by the command EXEC (member name). Thus, if a user has a CLIST named DATE in a partitioned dataset named 'userid.CLIST', the CLIST is executed by the command EXEC (DATE). The system assumes the CLIST type in an EXEC command, and the dataset does not have a qualifier name. Parentheses enclosing the member name are mandatory.

The reader should refer to additional discussion in Chapters 5 and 9 on executing CLISTs and the EXEC command.

4.3   CLIST PROCEDURE LIBRARIES

When the user enters a command for TSO, the system assumes a hierarchy of files for locating the command to be executed. Under normal conditions, presuming that the user has not modified the default for this hierarchy, the system will first search for the command in the system libraries. If that command is not found, it will search in the system CLIST libraries that are maintained by the computer facility.

Collectively, these system and facility files are most often allocated to the user's TSO session during logon using the file name SYSPROC. When the user has a partitioned dataset named 'userid.CLIST', it can also be allocated during logon under the name SYSPROC. If the user issues a command in TSO that the system cannot find in one of the system or facility libraries, it will also search the user's CLIST library.

Depending on the standard employed by the computer facility, the user's CLIST library may be a partitioned dataset named 'userid.CLIST'. Any of its members could be executed in TSO simply by entering only the name of the CLIST member. Thus, a member named DATE, for example, can be executed by issuing the simple command DATE.

The user should not give a name to a CLIST that duplicates the name of a TSO command or the name of members in facility-supported CLIST libraries.

4.4   USING EDIT OR ISPF

A CLIST file is created by any edit or utility facility that can create a sequential file. The easiest and most commonly used methods are the TSO EDIT or ISPF facilities. An editor enables simple data entry of the initial coding, facilitates statement modification during the testing phase, and aids in maintaining the CLIST file after it is placed in production.

Each CLIST statement, TSO command and subcommand must begin on a new line in the dataset. Multiple statements may not be coded on the same line.

A CLIST file must be a numbered dataset in order for the CLIST to be executable. The line numbers must be in the last eight columns of each line in fixed-length records or in the first eight columns in variable-length records. Line numbers must also be incremented in an ascending order.

Both native TSO EDIT and the ISPF Edit feature automatically provide for valid placement and incrementing of line numbers when the file is defined as a numbered dataset.

A CLIST file must not contain any blank records.

4.5   TESTING AND DEBUGGING

The same care used to develop a high-level language program must also be used to develop a CLIST. While a CLIST is much easier to design and code than many other languages, it must be thoroughly tested and debugged.

The CLIST language and interpreter offer several features to assist the user in testing and debugging a CLIST. A CONTROL statement is used to invoke these features and should always be used to test and debug the CLIST. Several options can be coded in the CONTROL statement to enable the user to monitor execution of CLIST statements and substitution of variables.

One or any number of CONTROL statements may be included in a CLIST. A CONTROL statement is most often coded as the first or second statement of a CLIST to set initial test and debug options; at any point later in the CLIST, CONTROL statements may be included to change those options.

A CONTROL statement is used in testing a CLIST by specifying that execution will continue or abort on an error condition; that error messages are to be displayed or suppressed; that execution waits for a user to respond to a request for input or continues without a response; and that CLIST commands or subcommands will be displayed either before or after values are substituted in variables but before execution.

The format of the CONTROL statement and the options that are used in testing and debugging is as follows. The default is underlined. Any of the options may be coded in any order in the CONTROL statement.

```
CONTROL    FLUSH / NOFLUSH
           MSG / NOMSG
           PROMPT / NOPROMPT
           LIST / NOLIST
           CONLIST / NOCONLIST
           SYMLIST / NOSYMLIST
```

These six operands define certain operating options to be in effect when the CONTROL statement is executed. They are:

FLUSH   Terminates execution of the CLIST if an execution error occurs

NOFLUSH   Enables execution to continue even if an execution error occurs

MSG   Displays system messages if an error occurs

NOMSG   Suppresses system error messages

PROMPT   Allows execution to continue only after a user has responded to a request for input

NOPROMPT   Continues execution of the next statement without waiting for a user response

LIST   Displays TSO commands/subcommands at the terminal, after symbolic substitution of their variables but before execution of the commands/subcommands; does not display CLIST commands

NOLIST   Suppresses display of TSO commands and subcommands

CONLIST   Displays only CLIST commands at the terminal after symbolic substitution but before execution of the command; does not display TSO commands or TSO subcommands

NOCONLIST   Suppresses display of CLIST commands

SYMLIST   Displays executable statements (CLIST commands and TSO commands/subcommands) before resolution of the variables and before execution of the statement

NOSYMLIST   Suppresses display of executable statements

The use of one or more operands provides a valuable tool for testing and debugging a CLIST. They enable the user to list actual statements as they will be executed.

The following sample CLIST is an example of using options to display actual operations and to control execution. For the moment, the other statements in the example may be ignored.

```
PROC 0
CONTROL FLUSH MSG PROMPT LIST CONLIST SYMLIST
WRITE ENTER ANY NUMBER FROM 1 TO 10
READ &A
SET &X EQ (&A * 5)
WRITE THE ANSWER IS &X
END
```

In this example, the user is prompted to enter a number from 1 to 10. This number is read by the READ statement and a new variable is set equal to the user's number multiplied by 5. The computed value is then displayed at the terminal by the WRITE statement. The procedure then terminates.

When the CLIST is executed, if an error occurs, execution is immediately terminated because of the FLUSH operand. If the operand NOFLUSH had been specified, the statement where the error occurred could not be executed although execution will continue at the next statement.

The use of FLUSH or NOFLUSH during testing may be useful for long CLIST procedures in particular. When a particular part of a CLIST is being tested to resolve an error, FLUSH may be used to bypass all operations that follow the statement that causes the error. This prevents operations which should not be executed if an error exists and reduces the test time.

The MSG operand causes the system to display system messages if an error occurs. If NOMSG was coded, system messages are not displayed. When testing, it is recommended that the MSG operand always be in effect.

The PROMPT operand enables display of system messages to ask a terminal user to supply necessary information omitted from a TSO command or subcommand in the CLIST. When this operand is specified as NOPROMPT, system messages to prompt for this information are inhibited. In a test environment, PROMPT is highly recommended. Most of the TSO commands or subcommands will fail when required parameters or other information have not been specified. NOPROMPT may be appropriate for a CLIST that is fully tested and in production and when the end user could not respond reliably to the system message. The CLIST should include error detection and processing routines.

In testing, it may be useful to bypass responses from a user when a particular value is not required. However, care must be used to ensure that variables are assigned values, or an error condition can occur. This might be accomplished by coding a temporary SET statement prior to the READ statement to assign a value to the variable. This SET statement would be removed after the applicable testing phase is completed.

The LIST, CONLIST and SYMLIST operands are the most valuable in testing a CLIST because they display the variables in the statements before they are executed.

When the sample CLIST from above is executed, each statement after the CONTROL statement is displayed at the terminal. In the listing below, lines shown in upper case are statements in the actual CLIST file; they are not displayed and are in the listing only to demonstrate the sequence of operations.

Lines shown in lower case are displayed by the LIST, CONLIST and SYMLIST operands.

The indented text labeled "display:" following the two WRITE statements is produced by the WRITE command; the messages are not affected by the CONTROL operands.

Note that the first two statements, PROC 0 and CONTROL, will not be displayed. Operands take effect only after a CONTROL statement is executed. The following example assumes that a user answers "8" to the WRITE request for a number.

```
PROC 0
CONTROL FLUSH MSG PROMPT LIST CONLIST SYMLIST
WRITE ENTER ANY NUMBER FROM 1 TO 10
      conlist: write enter any number from 1 to 10
      symlist: write enter any number from 1 to 10
      display: ENTER ANY NUMBER FROM 1 TO 10
READ &A
      conlist: read 8
      symlist: read &a
SET &X EQ (&A * 5)
      conlist: set 40 eq (8 * 5)
      symlist: set &x eq (&a * 5)
WRITE THE ANSWER IS &X
      conlist: write the answer is 40
```

```
      symlist: write the answer is &x
      display:       THE ANSWER IS 40
END
      conlist: end
      symlist: end
```

No displays were produced by the LIST operand of the CON-TROL statement since no TSO commands or subcommands are included.

Multiple CONTROL statements can be coded in a CLIST in order to turn operands on and off. For example, if the same CLIST had included a second CONTROL statement as shown in the list below, the display at the terminal would be different. Note that CONTROL statements do not have to repeat operands that are already in effect. It is necessary to encode only those operands that the user wishes to change because each option remains in effect until it is changed or the CLIST ends.

In the example below, the second CONTROL statement is listed by both the CONLIST and SYMLIST operands because the display is generated before the CONTROL statement is executed. Note that the WRITE statement is listed only by CONLIST since the SYMLIST operand was turned off and LIST does not display any CLIST statements.

```
PROC 0
CONTROL FLUSH MSG PROMPT LIST CONLIST SYMLIST
WRITE ENTER ANY NUMBER FROM 1 TO 10
      conlist: write enter any number from 1 to 10
      symlist: write enter any number from 1 to 10
      display: ENTER ANY NUMBER FROM 1 TO 10
READ &A
      conlist: read 8
      symlist: read &a
SET &X EQ (&A * 5)
      conlist: set 40 eq (8 * 5)
      symlist: set &x eq (&a * 5)
CONTROL NOSYMLIST
      conlist: control nosymlist
      symlist: control nosymlist
```

```
WRITE THE ANSWER IS &X
     conlist: write the answer is 40
     display: THE ANSWER IS 40
END
     conlist: end
```

While LIST, CONLIST and SYMLIST are valuable aids in testing a CLIST, caution in their use is advisable. They should normally be used only during development and testing of the CLIST. Once the CLIST is placed into production, the LIST, CONLIST and SYMLIST operands can either be deleted to allow the defaults NOLIST, NOCONLIST and NOSYMLIST to be in effect or they can be specifically coded. CONTROL statements that do not have other operands may be deleted.

LIST, CONLIST and SYMLIST operands list each statement that occurs while the operand is in effect. They might therefore generate large volumes of terminal displays, especially when more than one is in effect. A WRITE statement will generate three lines of display, by WRITE, CONLIST and SYMLIST.

The multiplicity of lines displayed at the terminal could be difficult to interpret and could diminish the value of these important features. It may be most advisable to select only one of the operands for any given test.

When testing of a CLIST is completed, these operands should be turned off. The resulting output from these features can be quite confusing for the end user.

As discussed later in Chapter 8, several system variables can be used to change the status of the CONTROL statement options. These are classified in this book as the system variables for CONTROL Command Values.

5

Executing CLISTs

A CLIST is an online file that can be executed in three ways in TSO: explicit execution, implicit execution or extended implicit execution. The manner in which a CLIST is executed depends on the dataset name of the CLIST file and on the method chosen by the user. User-specified parameters and certain system options may be invoked when the CLIST is executed.

5.1   EXEC COMMAND

A CLIST procedure is executed by the TSO command EXEC. This command is used only to execute CLIST procedures. It may be explicitly stated, as in EXEC dsname, which executes the CLIST file named in "dsname". This is known as explicit execution of a CLIST procedure.

A CLIST may be initiated by specifying only a member name in a partitioned dataset (PDS) of CLISTs. This is referred to as implicit execution of a CLIST procedure. The name of the member in a CLIST file is specified by the user and the term EXEC is implied. Implicit execution requires that the CLIST file be a member in a partitioned dataset that is allocated to the user's TSO session as a part of the SYSPROC file.

When implicit execution is used, the system searches for the name of the CLIST in the system TSO and CLIST libraries. If not found, it then searches in the user's CLIST library that is a partitioned dataset named 'userid.CLIST' and allocated to the file SYSPROC. Searches through system TSO libraries can be bypassed. The system can be instructed to search in the SYSPROC libraries only, thus reducing the time needed to locate the CLIST procedure. This is accomplished by the use of extended implicit execution.

5.1.1   Explicit Execution

Explicit execution of a CLIST refers to initiating the CLIST by issuing the TSO command EXECUTE, EXEC or EX. The command is followed by the dataset name of the CLIST file. This is followed by an optional list of "parameter" values that are assigned to variables, if any, specified on the initial PROC statement in the CLIST. Finally, two system operands may be included on an explicit EXEC command. Either LIST or NOLIST and either PROMPT or NOPROMPT can be specified.

The format of an explicit EX command follows.

```
EX dsname 'parameters' [LIST/NOLIST] [PROMPT/NOPROMPT]
```

The "dsname" may be the name of a sequential dataset or the name of a partitioned dataset with the member name enclosed in parentheses. The formats of dataset names are as shown.

```
'userid.CLIST'  'userid.X.CLIST'  'userid.PDS.CLIST(X)'
```

The string of one or more user-specified values, shown above as "parameters", must be enclosed in single quote marks. If more than one value is specified, the entire string must be enclosed within a pair of single quote marks as follows.

```
'variable1 variable2 variable3 variable4 variable5'
```

The system options LIST/NOLIST and/or PROMPT/NOPROMPT may be specified. Explicit execution is required if a user intends to specify either or both of these operands.

Explicit execution is also necessary if the name of the dataset does not end with the standard suffix CLIST as its type.

Finally, explicit execution is required to execute any CLIST not allocated to the SYSPROC file name for the TSO session.

5.1.2   Implicit Execution

Implicit execution refers to executing a CLIST when the EXEC command is implied. The implicit method of execution can be used only when the CLIST is a member within a user's command procedure library which is allocated to the SYSPROC library. The significant advantage of implicit execution is that the procedure can be executed simply by entering only the member name as though it is the name of a TSO command.

The format for implicit execution follows.

```
membername parameters
```

The term EXEC is implied and must not be coded. The name of a CLIST to be executed has to be the name of the PDS member. The full dataset name is not entered in the command. Thus, the dataset name for a user's private CLIST library must be 'userid.CLIST'.

A string of one or more user-specified values as parameters may be specified. They must not be enclosed in quote marks. Thus, implicit execution of a CLIST where the user specifies three variables would use the format shown here.

```
membername variable1 variable2 variable3
```

The default system options NOLIST and NOPROMPT are in effect automatically and cannot be overridden. Thus, LIST/NOLIST or PROMPT/NOPROMPT cannot be specified. However, the CLIST may contain a CONTROL statement to specify these operands.

5.1.3   Extended Implicit Execution

Extended implicit execution invokes a CLIST in the same way as implicit execution. The term EXEC is implied. The CLIST must be a member in the user's command library that must be named 'userid.CLIST' and allocated to the file SYSPROC.

A string of one or more user variables may be specified, but are not enclosed in quote marks. The system default options NOLIST and NOPROMPT are in effect and may not be overridden although they may be specified on a CONTROL statement.

When extended implicit execution is invoked, the system will bypass all the system TSO libraries and search for the named procedure only in the system and user CLIST libraries that are allocated to the SYSPROC file.

Extended explicit execution is the fastest method to locate and initiate a command procedure.

Extended implicit execution is invoked by using the format for implicit execution and including a percent sign (%) as a prefix to the membername. The format follows.

```
%membername variable1 variable2 variable3
```

5.2   SPECIFYING PARAMETERS IN EXEC COMMANDS

Parameters may be specified when a CLIST is initiated by the explicit, implicit or extended implicit methods. Parameters specify a list of one or any number of values. They are the actual values to be substituted for variables when the CLIST is first initiated. All values specified in an explicit or implicit EXEC command must be defined in the PROC statement. A PROC statement must be the first statement in the CLIST.

In the example below, both positional and keyword parameters are used. In this example, there are two positional and two keyword parameters that correspond to the variables defined on the PROC statement. This enables the user to specify the values for the variables when the CLIST is initiated.

```
EXEC (TEST) '100 ABC MONTH(DEC) YR(91)'
PROC 2 NUMB SEQ MONTH() YR(86)
```

5.2.1   Positional Parameters

Positional parameters must be defined on the PROC statement. The term positional describes this kind of parameter in that they must be coded on the PROC statement and must be entered on the EXEC command in a positional order. Substitution for variables occurs in the same positional order as specified on the PROC statement. Therefore, they must be given on the EXEC command in the same relative order.

The first operand after the term PROC must be the number of positional parameters. If no positional variables are used, the number must be "0". In the example above, there are two positional parameters, NUMB and SEQ. The value "100" in the EXEC statement is assigned to the first positional variable, NUMB. "ABC" is given to the second positional variable, SEQ.

If values are not specified by the user for each positional variable when the CLIST is initiated, the system will prompt the user for the missing values. Note that, since these are positional parameters, the system assumes that the values in the EXEC command are to be substituted for variables in the PROC statement in the same sequence.

The following examples demonstrate the symbolic substitution of variables with initial values when the CLIST is invoked.

```
EXEC (TEST) '100 ABC'
PROC 2 NUMB SEQ
```

The value of NUMB is "100" and the value of SEQ is "ABC".

```
EXEC (TEST) 'ABC 100'
PROC 2 NUMB SEQ
```

The value of NUMB is "ABC" and the value of SEQ is "100". An error condition may occur or, at least, this is not what was intended for the process.

```
EXEC (TEST) '100'
PROC 2 NUMB SEQ
```

The value of NUMB is "100". The system will prompt the user to enter a value for SEQ.

```
EXEC (TEST) 'ABC'
PROC 2 NUMB SEQ
```

The value of NUMB is "ABC". The system will prompt the user to enter a value for SEQ. As in the previous examples, the intent is that "ABC" be assigned to SEQ. However, these are positional parameters and the system assumes that the single value entered applies to the first variable.

```
EXEC (TEST)
PROC 2 NUMB SEQ
```

The system will prompt the user to specify a value for NUMB. When the user responds with a value, the system will prompt the user to enter a value for SEQ.

Whenever the system prompts the user for a positional value, a real value must be entered in response. A null entry will not be accepted and the system will merely repeat the prompt for a real value. A null entry is transmitted by using only the ENTER or RETURN key on the keyboard. A space (blank) is not a null value.

This is an important point. Many new TSO users enter only a null value by pressing the ENTER or RETURN key only. A null entry is rejected when it is entered in response to either a system prompt for a positional value as a CLIST is initiated or a system message requesting information needed to execute a TSO command or subcommand. As long as the new user issues null values, the system repeats the prompt. Most often, the system's patience is greater than the terminal user's.

5.2.2 Keyword Parameters

Keyword parameters are defined in a PROC statement following all positional parameters. If no positional parameters have been specified, the number "0" must be specified and keyword parameters follow this operand. Keyword parameters need not be specified in any particular sequence, either on the PROC statement or in the EXEC command. The values are associated with the specific variables by the name of the variable. In the following example, there are two keyword variables.

```
EXEC (TEST) 'MONTH(DEC) YEAR(91)'
PROC 0 MONTH(NOV) YEAR(90)
```

The value "DEC" is assigned to the variable MONTH because it is identified by that name in the EXEC statement. The value "91" is similarly assigned to the variable YEAR. The values given in the EXEC statement must be enclosed in parentheses and must be prefixed with the name of the variable.

Keyword variables may be given default values. In the above example, "NOV" and "90" are default values. The values "DEC" and "91" entered in the EXEC statement actually override the default values. If the user does not specify any value for a keyword variable on the EXEC statement, the default value remains in effect unless changed during CLIST execution.

Keyword variables may be designated without having a value. A keyword variable having a value of null, that is, having no value, is coded with only left and right parentheses with no space or any other characters, as follows.

```
PROC 0 MONTH( ) YEAR( )
```

If the user does not specify a value when the EXEC statement is issued, the keyword variable will initiate with no value. The system will not prompt the user for a value. Therefore, caution must be used when keyword variables are used without assigning an initial value. This problem can be resolved by testing the variable after the CLIST has started. Below are examples of keyword variables with a null default value.

```
EXEC (TEST) 'MONTH(DEC) YEAR(91)'
PROC 0 MONTH( ) YEAR( )
```

The value of MONTH is "DEC" and the value of YEAR is "91".

```
EXEC (TEST) 'MONTH(DEC)'
PROC 0 MONTH( ) YEAR( )
```

The value of MONTH is "DEC" and the value of YEAR is null.

```
EXEC (TEST) 'YEAR(91)'
PROC 0 MONTH( ) YEAR( )
```

The value of MONTH is null and the value of YEAR is "91".

```
EXEC (TEST)
PROC 0 MONTH() YEAR()
```

The value of both MONTH and YEAR is null.

```
EXEC (TEST) 'MONTH() YEAR()'
PROC 0 MONTH(DEC) YEAR(91)
```

In this example, the user has overridden the default values. Both MONTH and YEAR are null when the CLIST is initiated.

Keyword variables can also be defined and used for a special purpose. In this kind of application, keyword variables may be coded with no associated value—null or real. This kind of keyword variable serves as an "on" or "off" switch.

The capability for this special use of a keyword variable is available only in TSO/Extensions.

The PROC statement is coded normally except that the keyword variable is assigned no real or null value. In the following example, SWITCH is the name of the keyword variable.

```
PROC 0 MONTH(DEC) YEAR(91) SWITCH
```

When the user initiates the CLIST, the keyword variable name can be entered in the explicit or implicit EXEC command. If the name is entered with no associated value, the value will be set equal to the variable's name. When the user does not specify the name in the EXEC command, the keyword value will be set equal to null.

Therefore, using the above example of a PROC statement, when the user issues the following command

```
EXEC (TEST) 'MONTH(DEC) YEAR(91) SWITCH'
```

the value of the variable named SWITCH will be "SWITCH".

If the user enters the following EXEC command

```
EXEC (TEST) 'MONTH(DEC) YEAR(91)'
```

the value of the variable SWITCH will be null.

In both cases, the values "DEC" and "91" entered by the user will override the default values for MONTH and YEAR.

Within the CLIST, the value of the keyword variable could be tested to determine its value. Its value will either be the name of the variable or it will be null. Since there can be only two possible values for the variable, it can serve as a switch. The value can be tested as in the example shown here.

```
EXEC (TEST) 'MONTH(DEC) YEAR(91) SWITCH'
PROC 0 MONTH(DEC) YEAR(91) SWITCH
. . . . .
IF &SWITCH = SWITCH, THEN GOTO OPTION1
                     ELSE GOTO OPTION2
```

Another way to test if the value of a variable is null is to test its length, that is, determine the number of characters in the value. When the number of characters is 0, the value must be null since a null value has no characters. When the number of characters is any number greater than 0, the value must be real.

The following CLIST statement will determine the length of a value. The logic of the test is identical to that of the IF statement above. The IF statement is discussed in Chapter 9, and the system variable &LENGTH is presented in Chapter 8.

```
IF &LENGTH(&SWITCH) = 0, THEN GOTO OPTION1
                         ELSE GOTO OPTION2
```

5.2.3   System Operands LIST and PROMPT

The system-defined operands LIST/NOLIST and PROMPT/ NOPROMPT may be included with an EXEC command for explicit execution. They cannot be specified when the CLIST is invoked either by implicit or extended implicit execution although they can be specified on CONTROL statements within the CLIST.

These operands must follow the specification of user-defined parameters, if any. The format of the EX statement is shown here. The default operand is underlined.

```
EX dsname 'parameters' [LIST/NOLIST] [PROMPT/NOPROMPT]
```

The LIST operand displays at the user's terminal each of the TSO commands and/or subcommands in the procedure as they are executed. They are displayed after all symbolic substitution of variables. NOLIST prohibits the display and is the default. Using NOLIST does not affect the display of WRITE statements or other operational output. LIST does not display CLIST commands.

The PROMPT operand enables prompting messages to the user at a terminal during CLIST execution. NOPROMPT is the default. It suppresses prompting messages. When PROMPT is specified, LIST is also assumed unless NOLIST is specifically entered.

Each TSO user has a user profile maintained by the system to define certain characteristics for the user and the session. One of these attributes enables or disables prompting. When the user's profile specifies that prompting is disabled, all requests to use PROMPT are ignored. Thus, when prompting is inhibited, it cannot be overridden by specifying PROMPT in a CONTROL statement or in an EXEC command to initiate a CLIST.

5.3   SYSPROC AND LOGON PROCEDURES

CLIST procedure libraries and their inclusion in the SYSPROC file, as discussed in Chapter 4 and earlier in this chapter, offer a significant benefit to the TSO user. Most important of the advantages is the capability to execute a CLIST using the implicit and extended implicit form of the EXEC command.

When a user logs on to TSO, the system executes an automated logon procedure. This process performs certain routines to activate security, operational and other characteristics for the user's session. As a part of this logon procedure, the system will perform routines that allocate system libraries for the user so that he can execute TSO commands, invoke the ISPF and other system components, retrieve TSO's interactive help information and perform other interactive tasks.

One of the files allocated for the user's session has a file name of SYSPROC. Allocation of two or more system libraries is performed by the process referred to as concatenation.

Concatenation is the allocation of two or more physical datasets as a single logical file. Even though the datasets in a concatenated file are individual files, they are processed as a single logical file. Thus, for example, when libraries ABC and DEF are concatenated under a file name of, say, LIB, any members residing in either library are located simply by searching in the logical file having the file name LIB.

The system searches in concatenated libraries for the member in the same order as the datasets were identified when they were allocated. If the same member name occurs in more than one library concatenated under the same file name, the first occurrence of the member is retrieved, based on the order in which the libraries were allocated for concatenation.

Many computer facilities automatically concatenate a user's private CLIST library, when available, with system libraries under the file name SYSPROC. This is done during the system processing when logging on to TSO. The user's CLIST library must conform to computer facility standards. Normally, only one user library is included in the SYSPROC allocation. The CLIST library must be a partitioned dataset, usually with a dataset name of 'userid.CLIST', must be cataloged, and must reside on a permanently mounted disk volume.

Users' command procedure libraries are normally allocated as the last dataset after all of the system libraries.

By concatenation, a private CLIST library is included in the allocation of system libraries under the file name SYSPROC.

Inclusion of the user's command procedure library in SYSPROC enables that user to perform implicit and extended implicit execution of CLISTs in their 'userid.CLIST' library. If the library is not allocated to SYSPROC, only explicit execution of its CLIST members is possible.

5.4   CLISTS IN AUTOMATIC LOGON PROCEDURES

Most computer facilities also provide the capability, during the TSO logon, to execute procedures in the private library. These procedures could include such actions as allocation of specific files and datasets, execution of user programs and other routines, invocation of ISPF or other system features, or other user-defined tasks.

This capability enables automatic initiation of a "startup" CLIST immediately upon logging on to TSO. The user procedure must reside in a PDS CLIST library concatenated as a SYSPROC file during logon processing. One member in the library can be automatically executed during logon, provided the name of that member conforms to computer facility standards. Common names for startup CLIST procedures include "ON", "START" and "$STARTUP".

5.5 CONCATENATING USER AND SYSTEM LIBRARIES

A TSO user may need to change the datasets allocated as the SYSPROC file. Also, because the SYSPROC files are currently allocated and in use, they cannot be allocated for different purposes or under a different file name. When this occurs, the SYSPROC file must be freed or released and the datasets must be re-allocated.

In addition, a user may wish to add libraries to the SYSPROC files during the TSO session. Datasets can be added to the current SYSPROC file by re-allocating it. All datasets are named and the REUSE operand of the ALLOCATE command is coded to reuse any datasets currently allocated to SYSPROC. This avoids the necessity to first free and then re-allocate datasets that are currently allocated to SYSPROC.

The following TSO command is an example of concatenating two physical datasets, 'SYS1.CLIST' and a private library named 'userid.CLIST'. These two physical datasets are identified in the operand DATASET (DA). They are concatenated into the logical file identified by the file name SYSPROC in the FILE (FI) operand of the ALLOCATE command.

```
ALLOC FI(SYSPROC) DA('SYS1.CLIST' 'userid.CLIST') SHR
```

The user may re-allocate a SYSPROC file to change or remove datasets allocated to it. SYSPROC can also be re-allocated to change the sequence of dataset concatenation so that the system will search for a member in a given library first.

The user may re-allocate his or her own SYSPROC file by using the commands below. The commands must be executed each time the SYSPROC file is re-allocated. It is necessary to release or free the SYSPROC file before a new SYSPROC can be defined.

The commands to re-allocate a SYSPROC file are as follows.

```
FREE FI(SYSPROC)
ALLOC FI(SYSPROC) DA(list of dsnames) SHR
```

The terms FI, DA and SHR in these TSO commands are operands that refer to the symbolic FILENAME, the list of two or more DATASETs and a disposition of SHR (share) for the datasets.

If the user intends to only redefine SYSPROC with additional datasets, that is, if all currently allocated datasets are to remain in the SYSPROC definition, the SYSPROC file should not be freed. Rather, SYSPROC is defined by naming all of the datasets in the DA operand and entering the REUSE operand in the ALLOCATE command. The REUSE operand retains all of the datasets that are currently allocated.

The TSO ALLOCATE command to re-allocate the SYSPROC file and to reuse current dataset allocations is as follows.

```
ALLOC FI(SYSPROC) DA(list of dsnames) SHR REUSE
```

When the system accesses a dataset, it creates input/output buffers in memory for temporary storage of records when read and written. These I/O buffers significantly improve system performance in input and output operations. The size of the buffers is based on the physical block size of the dataset.

When multiple datasets are allocated as concatenated files, the system allocates the I/O buffers based on the block size of the first specified dataset. When the block size of the first dataset is smaller than another dataset, the buffers will be too small. Processing of the concatenated datasets will fail with a system abnormal termination.

Therefore, the dataset with the largest physical block size should be specified first in the list of datasets in the DA operand of the ALLOCATE command. If this is not possible or desirable because of the necessary sequence of searching the concatenated libraries, the BLKSIZE operand of the ALLOCATE must be specified. The value for the BLKSIZE operand has to be the size of the largest block size regardless of the size of the first dataset in the list.

The following example illustrates concatenation of datasets with different block sizes. Remember that a BLKSIZE operand is not necessary when all datasets have the same block size or the first dataset has the largest block size.

```
ALLOC FI(SYSPROC) DA(list of dsnames) SHR BLKSIZE(nnnn)
```

As an example, suppose that three libraries are concatenated with the file name SYSPROC. The dataset names and physical block sizes of these three libraries are listed in the order in which they are to be concatenated.

SYS1.CLIST	Block size = 6160
PROD.CLIST	Block size = 6000
userid.CLIST	Block size = 6320

The ALLOCATE command to concatenate these libraries is shown below. The plus sign at the end of each line only continues the command onto the next line. On the terminal, the entire command could be entered as one line. Note that the operand BLKSIZE specifies a value of 6320, which is the largest block size of the libraries even though 'userid.CLIST' is the last specified dataset.

```
ALLOC FI(SYSPROC) +
      DA('SYS1.CLIST','PROD.CLIST','userid.CLIST') +
      SHR +
      REUSE +
      BLKSIZE(6320)
```

5.6   CLISTS IN A BATCH JOB

CLISTs are normally executed in TSO in the interactive mode. The capability for the TSO user to interact with a procedure is perhaps the most significant advantage of this language.

On the other hand, batch processing is often far less costly than interactive processing to accomplish the same tasks. A batch job could be an effective and efficient way to perform any given set of tasks.

Performing the CLIST tasks in a batch job is most applicable when the CLIST executes a stable set of operations. The use of a CLIST in a batch job presumes that no user interface is needed or, at a minimum, that all "responses" to TSO command prompts and to CLIST queries are known in advance. In other words, the value of every variable must be included with the CLIST or on the EXEC command that invokes it. In addition, every TSO command and subcommand must be complete and values supplied for all of their required operands.

When these conditions are satisfied, executing CLISTs in the batch mode of processing can be the better solution.

In the batch job, TSO can be executed just as any other user program or system utility. Of course, the processing is not inter-active—there is no user interface. However, all TSO facilities and features are available, except the capability for interactive "dialog."

A CLIST to be executed in a batch job is performed by a step that must invoke the TSO program. The JCL for the job must include a valid EXEC statement to execute the TSO program as well as the DD (Data Definition) statements required by TSO. These DD state-ments define the input and the output files of the TSO program.

The following presents an example of the required JCL coding to execute TSO in a batch job. Since TSO is being executed, any TSO commands and subcommands may be included in the job. This includes the command EXEC to invoke a CLIST procedure.

```
//STEP     EXEC PGM=IKJEFT01
//SYSTSIN  DD   SYSIN DD *
tso commands
EXEC 'userid.CLIST(XYZ)' 'parameters'
tso commands
//SYSTSOUT DD   SYSOUT=A
//SYSPRINT DD   SYSOUT=A
```

In the example above, each line beginning with a // is a JCL statement. The // identifies the line as a JCL statement to the system. All lines that do not start with // are not JCL statements.

The JCL statement called STEP executes the program IKJEFT01, the IBM name for the TSO program.

The statement identified as SYSTSIN defines the dataset for input to the TSO program. The name SYSTSIN is the file name or DD name. Use of this name is mandatory and must be coded as shown. All TSO commands, including any EXEC command that executes a CLIST, must be contained in this input file.

The statements with the file names SYSTSOUT and SYSPRINT are the output print files where the output generated by the TSO commands and messages from the TSO program are routed. They are also required DD statements.

Any CLIST referred to in an EXEC statement must reside on an online disk volume. The CLIST may be stored in a sequential dataset or it may be a member in a partitioned dataset and the dataset must be cataloged.

These same requirements also apply to all nested CLISTs that may be invoked from within the main procedure.

5.7   EXERCISES

1. Which of the following statements about CLISTs are false? If not true, why not? What is the correct answer?

    _____ CLISTS must include one or more CLIST statements and at least one TSO command or subcommand.

    _____ The CLIST must be a sequential dataset or member of a partitioned dataset and must be line-numbered.

    _____ A CLIST with a non-standard dataset name may be invoked either by explicit or implicit execution, but not by extended implicit execution.

    _____ A CLIST may consist of only TSO subcommands.

    _____ The default values assigned to the positional and keyword parameters are null values.

2. Each CLIST statement below contains one or more structure and syntax errors. Correct all of the errors. Do not be concerned with any aspect of the statement except for its structure and syntax. Assume that all lines below are in the same CLIST but that this is only a partial list. The PROC statements in line 110 and line 175 define positional and keyword parameters, and values will be specified by a user when the CLIST is initiated. There are 20 errors.

```
040 SET &A = (&B+XYZ) ; GOTO LABELA

110 LABELA: PROC 2 VAR1 VAR2(ABC) VAR3(XYZ) VAR4
```

```
150 LABELB. WRITE ENTER YOUR NAME

175 PROC 0 &KYWD1() &KYWD2()

210 IF A EQ &B
    THEN GOTO 240

250 /* This is a Date routine

240 SET&DATASET =&DSN.DATA

275 SET &DATE &MONTH&DAY&1991

290 IF &X = &B, THEN GOTO LABEL5:
```

6

CLIST Processing Flow

The normal flow of processing in a CLIST begins at the first statement, and each consecutive statement in turn is executed until the last statement is executed.

Processing is terminated when the last statement in the file occurs or when an END or EXIT statement is executed. CLISTs will terminate abnormally if an error condition occurs or if the terminal user interrupts the processing.

The CLIST language has numerous capabilities that can alter this normal processing sequence. Branching commands, nested CLISTs, DO loops and subprocedures all can affect processing flow. Error conditions and attention interrupts by the user can be detected. Routines to handle these situations can be included in the CLIST, or processing may be continued. Finally, processing flow can be temporarily transferred to a user and then returned to the CLIST procedure.

6.1   SEQUENCE OF STATEMENT EXECUTION

Commands, subcommands and CLIST statements are executed in a sequential order. That is, processing begins with the first statement and proceeds to each successive statement until an EXIT or

END statement in the CLIST is executed or until the last statement in the procedure has been encountered.

Comments are not executable statements. Therefore, they cannot affect the sequence of execution nor may they be objects of any condition or statement that modifies the sequence of processing in the CLIST.

There are seven conditions or operations that may change the sequence of execution.

1. An unconditional branch to another point in the CLIST occurs when a GOTO statement is executed. The branch can be only to a statement that has a label.
2. A conditional branch to another point in the CLIST is executed as a result of a condition test performed by an IF–THEN–ELSE or a SELECT–WHEN–OTHERWISE statement. The branch occurs when a GOTO statement is the action to be executed either when an IF condition is true or false, or when a SELECT condition occurs. Processing may transfer to a labeled statement only.
3. Execution passes to a nested CLIST or other procedure when an EXEC statement is performed. When the nested procedure ends, processing continues at the statement after the EXEC statement in the higher-level CLIST.
4. Processing passes to a subprocedure included within a CLIST when a SYSCALL statement is executed. When the subprocedure ends, processing continues with the next statement after the SYSCALL statement.
5. Execution loops through one or more statements within a DO group. Processing of the statements in the loop can be controlled by limiting the number of times the loop is executed. DO groups can be executed one time only, a specified number of times, while a condition is true, or until a condition is false. Processing of a DO group can also depend on multiple conditions.
6. Control is passed to the terminal user when a TERMIN statement is executed. Processing is returned to the next statement in the CLIST when the user enters one of the character strings defined in TERMIN.
7. If an attention interrupt is entered by the TSO user, execution is passed to the action defined for an ATTN routine. The action may be either one TSO command or a DO group of one or more

CLIST statements. The ATTN routine may include an EXIT to terminate the CLIST or a RETURN statement to transfer processing back to the statement where the interrupt occurred.

When the system detects an error condition, execution is passed immediately to the statements defined in an ERROR routine. The action in an ERROR routine may be a single TSO command or CLIST statement or a DO group of any TSO commands and/or CLIST statements. An EXIT or a RETURN statement must be included in the action.

All of the commands, subcommands and other statements coded within the ATTN or ERROR DO group are executed. However, the DO group could include statements to end the CLIST or to branch out of the routine.

If a RETURN statement is encountered in the DO group, control is returned to the statement that follows the statement where the interrupt or error occurred.

If an ATTN or ERROR routine is not in effect when the interrupt or error condition occurs, the procedure is immediately terminated and control is returned to the terminal user in the TSO READY mode.

6.2   NESTED CLISTS

A CLIST may have an EXEC statement to execute another CLIST. This subordinate CLIST can also include EXEC statements that invoke CLISTs on an even lower level. They are referred to as nested CLISTs or nested procedures.

Nested CLISTs are used in performing hierarchical functions. A series of nested levels of CLISTs can be constructed in a manner similar to modular programming. Nesting can simplify test procedures, and enhances the potential for flexibility.

The command procedure invoked by the user in either explicit or implicit EXEC mode is the highest-level procedure in this hierarchy. All procedures invoked by a top-level CLIST are nested within it. Nested CLISTs may also invoke lower-level nested CLISTs.

Execution returns to the higher-level CLIST when the invoked CLIST ends or if an EXIT or END statement occurs. Execution in the parent CLIST continues at the statement following the EXEC command that invoked the subordinate procedure.

A procedure at any given level sets an execution environment (TSO command or subcommand) for that level and at all levels below it. Nested CLISTs invoked at the subcommand level may execute only TSO subcommands and CLIST statements. They may not contain TSO commands. For example, a command procedure that performs the TSO EDIT command may invoke a nested CLIST when in the EDIT mode. However, the nested CLIST as well as any subordinate CLIST procedure that it may invoke may only execute EDIT subcommands and/or CLIST statements.

Each invocation of a nested procedure gets a new copy of the procedure. This means that, when a parent procedure invokes a subordinate CLIST, the system does not retrieve an earlier or existing copy of the nested CLIST but a fresh copy of it. Therefore, when a nested procedure is re-executed, values in variables in the nested CLIST that were assigned in previous executions are no longer available and must be reassigned.

6.3   PASSING VARIABLES TO NESTED CLISTS

Values can be passed to and from variables in a nested CLIST by the definition of global variables. Global variables may be used anywhere in the main CLIST and in any nested CLISTs.

A required GLOBAL statement in the main CLIST defines all of the global variables. A GLOBAL statement must also be coded in each nested procedure that will use the global variables.

Values that will be passed to a nested CLIST must be set for all applicable global variables before the parent procedure executes the EXEC statement to invoke the nested procedure.

Values that will be returned to the parent CLIST must be set before the nested CLIST terminates.

Global variables are discussed in depth in Chapter 8, and the GLOBAL statement is examined in detail in Chapter 9.

All system variables are considered global and are therefore universally available in any main or nested CLIST procedure.

6.4   CLIST SUBPROCEDURES

Subprocedures may be included within a CLIST. Subprocedures can be invoked from any point in a main or a nested CLIST by executing a SYSCALL statement.

The feature to define and execute subprocedures is available only in TSO/Extensions.

Subprocedures ensure a modular or hierarchical structure for CLISTs similar to techniques used in structured programming. Subprocedures enable development of a simple main processing flow that invokes subordinate routines when they are needed. Moreover, any given subprocedure can be invoked at any point in the primary processing structure. It can be executed any number of times as it is needed to accomplish a given set of operations.

Subprocedures must be identified by a PROC statement. (This is not the same as the PROC statement that defines a CLIST.) The subprocedure PROC statement must have a label that also assigns a name to the subprocedure.

All statements comprising the CLIST subprocedure must follow the PROC statement. The subprocedure must be closed with an END statement.

The subprocedure can be called from any point in the primary CLIST by executing a SYSCALL statement. A SYSCALL statement must have as its first operand the name of the subprocedure. This name is defined by the label on the subprocedure's PROC statement.

When execution of a subprocedure ends, processing returns to the statement in the primary procedure immediately after the SYSCALL statement.

6.5   PASSING VARIABLES TO SUBPROCEDURES

Values can be passed to a subprocedure as parameters entered on the SYSCALL statement. The parameters are defined on the PROC statement for the subprocedure.

The function, format and operands of a SYSCALL statement are similar to an EXEC statement. The EXEC statement executes a CLIST and can pass values as parameters to variables defined on the CLIST's PROC statement. The same process applies for the SYSCALL statement to call a subprocedure and pass values to variables defined on the subprocedure's PROC statement.

The function, format and operands of a PROC statement in the subprocedure are similar to a PROC statement for a CLIST. A PROC statement in either a CLIST or a subprocedure specifies positional and/or keyword parameters. It must also indicate the number of positional parameters which could be zero.

Normally, variables named on the PROC and SYSCALL statements are used to pass values to a subprocedure. Even though the subprocedure may access and modify these variables, modified variables cannot be returned to the primary CLIST.

However, when a variable is also named in a SYSREF statement within the subprocedure, a value assigned to the variable by the subprocedure is available to the primary CLIST when the subprocedure ends. SYSREF statements may be included within any subprocedure.

In addition to the facility to pass values to a subprocedure as parameters, global variables may be defined by an NGLOBAL statement in the primary CLIST. Variables defined as "named global" variables are available in the primary CLIST and all subprocedures. Since user variables cannot be passed to or received from a subprocedure, variables that are to be used in one or more subprocedures must be defined by the NGLOBAL statement before any subprocedure is invoked. The values in NGLOBAL variables can be passed to, received from and shared between any of the CLIST procedures.

Subprocedure variables are discussed in detail in Chapter 8. The PROC, SYSCALL, SYSREF and NGLOBAL statements are covered thoroughly in Chapter 9.

6.6   NESTED CLIST AND SUBPROCEDURE ENVIRONMENTS

When a nested CLIST is executed and when a subprocedure is invoked, the current environment, defined either by a CONTROL statement in the primary CLIST or by default if no CONTROL statement was executed, is in effect for the nested CLIST or subprocedure.

If a CONTROL statement is executed in the nested CLIST or subprocedure, the new CONTROL options are in effect. However, when processing returns to the parent CLIST as the nested CLIST or subprocedure ends, CONTROL operands defined in the parent procedure are again in effect.

In summary, a CONTROL environment is passed to a nested

CLIST or subprocedure, but CONTROL options defined in a nested CLIST or subprocedure are not passed back to the parent procedure.

Similarly, ATTN and ERROR routines are passed to nested CLISTs and subprocedures. However, if the nested CLIST or subprocedure executes a new ATTN or ERROR statement, the new definition is activated. When the nested CLIST or subprocedure ends, any ATTN or ERROR routines in the parent CLIST are in effect again. Routines in a nested CLIST or subprocedure are not passed back to the parent even when the parent has no ATTN or ERROR routines.

To summarize, ATTN and ERROR routines are passed to the nested CLIST or subprocedure, but routines defined in a subordinate procedure are not returned to the parent.

Arithmetic, Comparison and Logical Operators

The CLIST language offers an extensive array of arithmetic, comparison and logical operators. They provide capabilities to perform arithmetic operations, to compare expressions and conditions, and to connect conditional tests.

7.1 ARITHMETIC OPERATORS

Arithmetic operators allow fixed-point arithmetic operations on numeric operands. The operands may be explicit numeric values, numeric symbolic variables, or any valid combination of numbers and variables. The operators are listed here.

+ Addition
− Subtraction
* Multiplication
/ Division
** Exponentiation
// Remainder

Arithmetic operations are performed after symbolic variables have been resolved. Then arithmetic operations are computed in a priority order. Positive and negative signs for values are evaluated first. Exponentiation and remainders are then computed. Third, multiplication and division are performed. Addition and subtraction are performed last.

Operands and operators as well as entire expressions may be enclosed in parentheses to control the order of operations. Computations are performed first on any expressions enclosed within the innermost parentheses. Computations for the next higher level are performed next and so on, until the highest-level expressions in the outermost parentheses are computed.

The use of parentheses often results in different values for a given expression. In the first line in the example below, the multiplication of 2 and 3 is performed first and then 4 is added to the interim result of 6. In the second example, the use of parentheses forces the addition of 3 and 4 first. Then the interim result of 7 is multiplied by 2.

```
2*3+4          equals 10
2*(3+4)        equals 14
```

Operators may be set off by one or more spaces or there may be no spaces. Either following example is correct, although the clarity of the expression is enhanced by the use of spaces.

```
(42+(63/3))    or    (42 + (63 / 3))
((&A/&B)-&C)   or    ((&A / &B) - &C)
```

7.2   COMPARISON OPERATORS

Comparison operators determine the comparative relationship between two values and/or expressions. The operators can be used only in IF–THEN–ELSE, DO–END, SELECT–WHEN–OTHERWISE and WHEN SYSRC statements.

There are eight comparison operators as listed here. They may be coded either as symbols or letters.

```
EQ    or    =     Equal
GT    or    >     Greater Than
```

LT	or	<	Less Than
NE	or	~=	Not Equal
NG	or	~>	Not Greater Than
NL	or	~<	Not Less Than
LE	or	<=	Less Than or Equal
GE	or	>=	Greater Than or Equal

The operator LE is logically equivalent to NG. The operator GE is logically equivalent to NL.

Symbol comparison operators may be preceded and followed by one or more or by no spaces. Letter operators must have one or more spaces before and after the operator. The following examples demonstrate the use of comparison operators and the requirements for spaces.

These three statements are identical in meaning

```
SET &A = &B + (&C * 10)
SET &A=&B + (&C * 10)
SET &A EQ &B + (&C * 10)
```

and these three statements are identical in meaning.

```
IF &A = &B, THEN .....
IF &A=&B, THEN .....
IF &A EQ &B, THEN .....
```

These examples show Less Than and Not Equal symbol operators.

```
DO WHILE &A < &B
DO WHILE &A~=&B
```

while these show Equal and Greater Than letter operators.

```
WHEN SYSRC(EQ 3) .....
WHEN SYSRC(GT 12) .....
```

Note that the only valid operators in SET statements are the symbol operator = or the letter operator EQ. Of course, SET is an assignment statement and not a comparison statement.

7.3   LOGICAL OPERATORS

Logical operators connect expressions in the test conditions for IF–THEN–ELSE, DO–WHILE–END, DO–UNTIL–END and SELECT–WHEN statements. They are used when multiple expressions are the object of the test. The result of comparisons may be either true or false. Logical operators may be letters or symbols.

```
AND    or    &&
OR     or    |
```

The symbol operators && and | may be set off by one or more, or by no spaces. The letter operators AND and OR must have one or more spaces both before and after the operator. Each of the following examples is correct.

```
IF  &A=&B|&A=&C
IF  &A=&B | &A=&C
IF  &A=&B OR &A=&C
```

The following example is not correct because the variable &B is interpreted as a variable name of &BOR and the OR operand is lost.

```
IF  &A=&BOR&A=&C
```

When multiple comparisons are used in an IF statement, each must be separated by a logical operator. Moreover, when the same expression is used in two or more comparisons, it must be explicitly repeated in each of the comparisons. Neither expressions nor operators may be implied.

The IF statements

```
IF  &A = &B OR &A = &C
IF  &A = &B OR &B = &C
```

are correct, but the statements

```
IF  &A = &B OR &C
IF  &A = &B OR &B &C
```

are not correct and will result in a syntax error.

The IF statement

```
IF &A = &B AND &A = &C
```

is correct, but the statement

```
IF &A = &B AND &C
```

is not correct and will result in a syntax error.

Variables

A symbolic variable is any named single item that symbolizes a real value, that is, a symbolic name in a CLIST for which an actual value is substituted when the name is evaluated.

Symbolic variables are usually identified by an ampersand as a prefix. For example, &A and &DATE are symbolic variables. However, the variable name on an OPENFILE, GETFILE, PUTFILE, CLOSFILE or PROC statement must not begin with the ampersand even though it must have an ampersand when used in any other statement.

8.1 TYPES OF VARIABLES

There are two broad categories of variables. They are user and system variables.

User variables are named and defined by a CLIST writer. The name of the user variable must not be the same as a reserved system variable name. The purposes of user variables are to store interim and final results, to perform calculations and logical relationships, to provide temporary storage for dataset and terminal input/output, and to pass or receive values for CLISTs and subprocedures.

There are three special ways that user variables are used.

Parameters	— Enable a terminal user to enter values as the CLIST is initiated; also pass values to a CLIST subprocedure when it is invoked.
Global	— Pass values to and receive values from one or more nested CLISTs and/or CLIST subprocedures.
Input/Output	— Read records from and write records to an opened disk dataset; also accept input from the terminal user.

System variables are established by the operating system and have system-reserved names. There are 61 system variables. System variables enable a user to determine much information about the host system operating environment, the user's datasets, and the status of CLIST execution. They are also used for a working area for input from the user's terminal.

Built-in functions are special system variables that enable the user to evaluate an associated expression. For example, a character string could be examined to determine whether it is numeric or character data. There are 11 system built-in functions.

8.2   USER VARIABLES

A user variable is any item named by the user that can take on any value assigned by the user. The variable name may be from 1 to 252 characters. However, variable names on a PROC statement may not exceed 31 characters, and the names of ISPF panel variables may not exceed 8 characters. Thus, variable names of 1 to 8 characters are highly recommended.

The first character must be a letter; the name is usually prefixed by an ampersand. The name for a user variable must not duplicate any name reserved for the system.

User variables must be defined in a SET, READ, PROC, GLOBAL, NGLOBAL, READDVAL or OPENFILE statement.

In the following example, &QUANTITY, &PRICE and &TOTSALE are user variables. &SYSDATE and &SYSDVAL are system variables.

```
WRITE THE DATE OF TODAY IS &SYSDATE
WRITENR ENTER THE NUMBER OF ITEMS SOLD ----->
```

```
READ
SET &QUANTITY EQ &SYSDVAL
WRITENR ENTER THE UNIT PRICE --------------->
READ
SET &PRICE EQ &SYSDVAL
SET &TOTSALE EQ (&QUANTITY * &PRICE)
WRITE THE TOTAL AMOUNT OF THE SALE IS ----> $&TOTSALE
```

The user would see the following terminal display and would enter responses to the requests for the number of items sold and for the unit price. The user's responses are 50 and 3.

```
THE DATE OF TODAY IS mm/dd/yy
ENTER THE NUMBER OF ITEMS SOLD ----->50
ENTER THE UNIT PRICE --------------->3
THE TOTAL AMOUNT OF THE SALE IS ----> $150
```

Because the two READ statements above do not name a variable where the user's input is to be stored, the input values are stored in the system variable named &SYSDVAL. Following the READ statements, the user variables &QUANTITY and &PRICE are set to the values in &SYSDVAL.

Alternatively, the READ statements could have identified the two user variables as shown below. The input data will then be stored in the variables identified on the READ statements and not in &SYSDVAL. Also, if this method had been selected to accept the user's input, the SET statements after the two READ statements would be omitted.

```
READ &QUANTITY
READ &PRICE
```

8.3   PARAMETERS

User variables may be defined and used as parameters to pass values to a CLIST when it is initiated by either an explicit or implicit EXEC command. The CLIST may be a main procedure initiated from TSO or may be a nested procedure initiated in an executing CLIST.

User variables may also be defined and used as parameters to pass values to a subprocedure within the CLIST. Values must be determined before the subprocedure is invoked. A SYSCALL statement invokes the subprocedure and names the variables.

8.3.1 Parameters for CLIST Execution

Variables used as parameters allow the CLIST user to specify values for predefined variables upon initiation of a CLIST. These are specified as the EXEC command is given to initiate the CLIST. The EXEC command may be issued in TSO READY mode or as a command within a CLIST to invoke a nested CLIST. In both cases, parameters may be included in the EXEC command.

A PROC statement must be the first statement in the CLIST if values are to be supplied by the user upon CLIST initiation. The PROC statement is required to define the variables. The variables may be either positional or keyword.

Positional variables are entered on the PROC statement in a sequential order, and a user must enter a value for each one in the same relative order as in the PROC statement. A PROC statement must include, as the first operand, the number of positional variables. If no positional variables are used, the first operand on the PROC statement must be "0".

Keyword variables may be entered on a PROC statement in any order after the number operand and all positional variables. Each keyword variable must be given a unique name, and a pair of parentheses that enclose a default value must immediately follow. The default value may be null; this is specified by a pair of parentheses with no value, as in (). When the user initiates the CLIST, the default value may be overridden by specifying on the EXEC statement the variable name and a new value enclosed in parentheses. The new value may be a null. The user may elect to accept a default value by not entering the variable name and value. Note that the user cannot see the default values defined for keyword parameters before the CLIST is invoked. Therefore, thorough documentation must be provided for those who will use CLISTs that include keyword parameters.

The following examples demonstrate that positional, keyword, both or no variables can be specified in the PROC statement. The user must supply a value for every positional parameter and has the option to specify a value or accept the default for keyword variables.

In this example, a PROC statement is coded but variables are not used. The number of positional variables must be "0".

```
EXEC (ABC)

PROC 0
```

In the following example, two positional variables are used. The user responds only to the first on the EXEC statement so that the system prompts the user for the second. Note that the parameter is enclosed in single quote marks on the EXEC statement but that the response to the prompt is not.

```
EXEC (ABC) 'DECEMBER'
      system: enter value for year
      user:   1991

PROC 2 MONTH YEAR
```

In the following example, there are no positional variables but there are five keyword variables. The user accepts default values for MONTH, YEAR and HOUR and overrides the values for DATE and MINUTE. The user has specified a null as the value for MINUTE and "25" for DATE. The null value for HOUR given on the PROC statement is not altered. The keyword variables on the EXEC statement may be given in any order.

```
EXEC (ABC) 'MINUTE() DATE(25)'

PROC 0 MONTH(DEC) DATE(15) YEAR(91) HOUR() MINUTE(15)
```

The following example demonstrates using both positional and keyword parameters. The user must enter a value for each of the positional variables first and may choose to override or accept the default values for the keyword variables. A user cannot see the default values of keyword variables.

```
EXEC (ABC) '12 30 DATE(25)'

PROC 2 HOUR MINUTE MONTH(DEC) DATE(15) YEAR(1991)
```

8.3.2   Parameters for Subprocedure Execution

The CLIST may also include subprocedures. Subprocedures may be invoked from any point within the CLIST. A subprocedure must begin with a PROC statement and must be terminated with an END statement. Any executable statements including CLIST statements, TSO commands and TSO subcommands may be included in the subprocedure. When the subprocedure is executed by a SYSCALL statement, all of its statements are executed.

Values may be passed to the subprocedure upon its initiation in the same manner that values may be passed to a CLIST when it is executed. Values passed to the subprocedure are coded on the SYSCALL statement that calls the subprocedure.

The first line in the subprocedure must be a PROC statement. The PROC statement is required whether variables are defined or not.

The PROC statement for subprocedures has the same format and function as the PROC statement for the main CLIST. It has a number to specify the count of positional parameters. When no positional parameters are defined, the count must be "0". The PROC statement may define one or multiple positional and keyword variables. Optionally, no variables may be defined.

The following example illustrates invoking a subprocedure in which there are one positional and two keyword parameters.

```
.....
SYSCALL SUB1 25 RATE(7) DEPT(ADMIN)
.....
.....
SUB1: PROC 1 QUANT RATE(5) DEPT(HQ)
      .....
      .....
      END
```

8.4   GLOBAL VARIABLES

Global variables are user variables that are defined for use in any one or more nested CLISTs and/or subprocedures. When a value is assigned to a global variable, that value is also available to all nested CLISTs or to all subprocedures.

A GLOBAL statement defines variables for nested CLISTs, while an NGLOBAL statement defines variables for subprocedures. A variable defined on a GLOBAL statement for nested CLISTs may not be used in subprocedures. Similarly, a variable defined on an NGLOBAL statement is not available to nested CLISTs.

If the nested CLIST or subprocedure modifies the value, that altered value remains in effect when the nested CLIST or the subprocedure ends.

All system variables are global and are therefore accessible in any level of nested CLIST and in all subprocedures.

8.4.1   Global Variables for Nested CLISTs

Global variables are used to transfer values between various levels of nested CLISTs. That is, values assigned to global variables are available in the main CLIST and in every level of nested CLISTs.

A GLOBAL statement must be coded in the highest-level CLIST. Each nested CLIST that uses any of the global variables must also include a GLOBAL statement, whereas a nested CLIST that does not refer to any of the specified global variables does not require a GLOBAL statement.

Variables coded on a GLOBAL statement are positional. They are accessed strictly by their relative position in a GLOBAL statement. Names of the global variables may be the same or different in the GLOBAL statements in the CLISTs. However, it is suggested that the same variable be given an identical name throughout all CLISTs to avoid any possible confusion.

The GLOBAL statement in the highest-level CLIST must specify all of the global variables. GLOBAL statements in the lower-level nested CLISTs need to define only those variables that it will use. However, since global variables are positional in nature, each variable that precedes the relative position of the required variables must also be included.

The following example demonstrates the coding required for using global variables. In this example, the CLIST at the first level is named MAIN. It invokes a nested CLIST named SECOND from the second level that, in turn, invokes a nested CLIST named THIRD from the third level.

"MAIN CLIST"
```
GLOBAL VAR1 VAR2 VAR3 VAR4 VAR5
SET &VAR1 = 10
SET &VAR2 = 10
SET &VAR3 = 30
SET &VAR5 = 50
EXEC SECOND
SET &TOTAL = VAR1 + VAR2 + VAR3 + VAR4 + VAR5
WRITE The Total is &TOTAL
EXIT
```

"SECOND CLIST"
```
GLOBAL VAR1 VAR2 VAR3 VAR4
SET &VAR3 = 30
SET &VAR4 = 40
EXEC THIRD
EXIT
```

"THIRD CLIST"
```
GLOBAL VAR1 VAR2
SET &VAR2 = &VAR2 * 2
EXIT
```

In the example above, the passing and receiving of variables between the three CLISTs occurs as follows.

- MAIN defines all global variables and then sets a value for VAR1, VAR2, VAR3 and VAR5. VAR4 remains null. The values VAR1 = 10, VAR2 = 10, VAR3 = 30 and VAR4 = null are passed onto SECOND. Although VAR1 and VAR2 are not used in SECOND, they have to be specified on the GLOBAL statement in SECOND because VAR2 is passed to THIRD and to ensure that VAR3 and VAR4 variables are in the third and fourth relative positions. VAR5 is not used either in SECOND or THIRD and is thus not defined in either.

- SECOND receives VAR1, VAR2, VAR3 and VAR4 from MAIN. It computes values for VAR3 and VAR4. It passes both VAR1 and VAR2 to THIRD but it does not use them. Its GLOBAL statement must include VAR1 so that the other variables retain their relative positions. Variable VAR2 must be specified so that it can be passed to THIRD.
- THIRD receives the variables VAR1 and VAR2 but does not use VAR1. VAR2 is multiplied by 2, giving it a value of 20. When THIRD ends with the EXIT statement, it passes the values 10 for VAR1 and 20 for VAR2 to SECOND.
- SECOND receives VAR1 and VAR2 from THIRD. It ends with its EXIT statement. SECOND returns to MAIN the values 10 for VAR1, 20 for VAR2, 30 for VAR3 and 40 for VAR4.
- MAIN receives four values from SECOND. Using these and the value of 50 it set for VAR5, it computes a variable named &TOTAL as the sum of all five variables. This is a value of 150. The WRITE statement then displays the message "The Total is 150". Processing ends with EXIT.

It is recommended that the GLOBAL statement in the top-level CLIST be copied to all nested CLISTs. This ensures that the same name is used in each reference to the variable and that all variables are in the correct relative position.

8.4.2   Global Variables for Subprocedures

Global variables are also used to pass values between a main or nested CLIST and a subprocedure within the CLIST. Values may be assigned before the subprocedure is invoked although this is not required. The values in global variables may be modified in the subprocedure. The changed value is returned to the CLIST that invoked the subprocedure.

Global variables for subprocedures are defined on an NGLOBAL statement. The term NGLOBAL means Named Global. NGLOBAL is quite different from a GLOBAL statement, which defines global variables for nested CLISTs.

The variable names defined on NGLOBAL statements are keyword parameters, not positional. Therefore, the list of variable names may be coded in any order; that is, the variable will be identified by its name, not its relative position, so that the sequence is not material. Moreover, no count of defined names is coded.

Every reference to a global variable on an NGLOBAL statement must refer to the name assigned to the variable.

When multiple levels of nested subprocedures are coded, that is, when a subprocedure includes a SYSCALL statement to call a nested subprocedure, subordinate procedures may include an NGLOBAL statement. The names of these global variables must be different from variable names on higher-level statements.

The following demonstrates the use of NGLOBAL variables in a CLIST procedure.

```
      NGLOBAL &VAR1
      SET &VAR1 = 40
      SYSCALL SUB1
      . . . . .
      . . . . .
SUB1: SET &VAR1 = 10 * &VAR1
```

8.5 INPUT/OUTPUT VARIABLES

User-defined variables may be used for receiving input that has been transmitted by a terminal user. The user's data is read into the user variables identified on a READ statement. A WRITE or WRITENR statement is used to transmit messages or other information to a terminal user.

User-defined variables are also used to receive records read from an open online dataset and to send records written to an open online dataset. When an input record is read, the system stores the record into the user variable named on the GETFILE statement. Before an output record is written, data is stored in a user variable named on the PUTFILE statement.

8.5.1 Terminal Input Variables

Input from a terminal user is received by a READ statement. Output to the terminal user is transmitted by either a WRITE or a WRITENR statement.

Operands on a READ statement, when used, are user variables. The READ statement nearly always immediately follows a WRITE or WRITENR statement to send a message to explain a required user response. The user may enter one or more answers based on the number of READ statement variables. The user's input is stored in the user variables named on the READ statement.

Alternatively, when a variable is not specified on the READ statement, the response is stored in a system variable named &SYSDVAL. The one or more values in &SYSDVAL may be read by a READDVAL statement to store them in user variables.

The operand on the WRITE or WRITENR statement is a character string that could include any characters, expressions and/or variables to form a message to be sent to the terminal user. The values of variables are displayed on the terminal.

The following example writes a message to a terminal user to request an answer. The user response is read into the user variable name specified on the READ statement.

```
WRITE Enter A Number From 1 To 5
READ &NUMBER
```

The following example executes the same process except that a user variable is not specified on the READ statement. The user response is stored in the system variable &SYSDVAL.

```
WRITE Enter A Number From 1 To 5
READ
READDVAL &NUMBER
```

8.5.2   Dataset Input/Output Variables

Input records are read from a dataset by GETFILE statements, while output records are written by PUTFILE statements. The file must reside on an online disk. It must be opened by an OPENFILE statement before any records can be read, and closed by a CLOSFILE statement when the I/O operation is completed. Only a sequential dataset or a member of a partitioned dataset may be processed by the CLIST language.

Records can be read only when an existing dataset is opened as

INPUT. Records may be written to an existing or new dataset opened as OUTPUT. If an existing online file is opened as UP-DATE, records may be read, updated and rewritten in the same location in the dataset.

Each time the GETFILE statement is executed, an input record is read. The contents of the input record are stored in the user variable named on the GETFILE statement. The contents of the output record must be stored in the variable named on the PUTFILE statement before the statement is executed. The contents of the user variable are written to the dataset by executing the PUTFILE statement.

Normally, GETFILE and PUTFILE statements are included within a loop so that multiple records are read, updated or written by the same CLIST statements. Of course, processing for the contents of the records must be included in the loop.

The same variable name must be specified for every OPENFILE, GETFILE, PUTFILE or CLOSFILE statement for a given dataset. The name is the ddname specified as the filename (FI) on the TSO command that allocated the dataset. It is the symbolic name assigned to the file, not the physical name of the dataset. If multiple files are open concurrently, each dataset must have a unique file name. In the example shown here, INFILE is the ddname assigned to the physical dataset "ABC.DATA".

```
ALLOCATE FI(INFILE) DA(ABC.DATA)
```

The following example illustrates dataset input and output. Only the first record is read from the file FILEIN, the date from the system variable &SYSDATE is appended to the record, and the modified record is written to the file FILEOUT.

```
OPENFILE FILEIN INPUT          /* Open input FILEIN    */
OPENFILE FILEOUT OUTPUT        /* Open output FILEOUT  */
GETFILE FILEIN                 /* Read FILEIN record   */
SET &FILEIN=&FILEIN&SYSDATE    /* Append current date  */
SET &FILEOUT=&FILEIN           /* Set output record    */
PUTFILE FILEOUT                /* Write FILEOUT record */
CLOSFILE FILEIN                /* Close input FILEIN   */
CLOSFILE FILEOUT               /* Close output FILEOUT */
```

8.6   SYSTEM VARIABLES

A system variable is defined by the system and is identified by a reserved name. There are 61 system variables, which may be categorized into seven functional classifications.

- Date and Time—5 System Variables

```
&SYSDATE        &SYSJDATE        &SYSSDATE
&SYSTIME        &SYSSTIME
```

- CPU Utilization—2 System Variables

```
&SYSCPU         &SYSSRV
```

- Host Environment—5 System Variables

```
&SYSHSM         &SYSISPF         &SYSLRACF
&SYSRACF        &SYSTSOE
```

- Terminal and User—5 System Variables

```
&SYSUID         &SYSPREF         &SYSPROC
&SYSLTERM       &SYSWTERM
```

- CLIST Execution—12 System Variables

```
&LASTCC         &MAXCC           &SYSDVAL
&SYSDLM         &SYSSCAN         &SYSOUTTRAP
&SYSOUTLINE     &SYSENV          &SYSICMD
&SYSPCMD        &SYSSCMD         &SYSNEST
```

- CONTROL Command Values—7 System Variables

```
&SYSASIS        &SYSFLUSH        &SYSMSG
&SYSPROMPT      &SYSLIST         &SYSCONLIST
&SYSSYMLIST
```

- Dataset Information—25 System Variables

&SYSDSNAME	&SYSVOLUME	&SYSUNIT
&SYSDSORG	&SYSRECFM	&SYSLRECL
&SYSBLKSIZE	&SYSKEYLEN	&SYSALLOC
&SYSUSED	&SYSPRIMARY	&SYSSECONDS
&SYSUNITS	&SYSEXTENTS	&SYSCREATE
&SYSEXDATE	&SYSREFDATE	&SYSUPDATED
&SYSPASSWORD	&SYSRACFA	&SYSADIRBLK
&SYSUDIRBLK	&SYSMEMBERS	&SYSTRKSCYL
&SYSBLKSTRK		

In addition, there are 11 system built-in functions. System functions evaluate a related character string or expression. The result of that evaluation is stored in a system variable whose name is the name of the built-in function. The system built-in functions are listed below.

&SYSDSN	&DATATYPE	&SYSCAPS
&SYSLC	&EVAL	&LENGTH
&STR	&NRSTR	&SYSNSUB
&SUBSTR	&SYSINDEX	

8.6.1   Date and Time

This group of system variables contains the current date and time from the system clock. They are often used in terminal displays. The month, day and year can be extracted from the current date. The hour, minute and seconds can be extracted from the current time.

The only difference in the variables &SYSDATE, &SYSJDATE and &SYSSDATE and in the variables &SYSTIME and &SYSSTIME is in their formats.

None of the date and time variables can be modified.

&SYSDATE

&SYSDATE contains the current system date. Its value is an eight-character alphanumeric date of the form MM/DD/YY where MM is the two-digit month, DD is the two-digit day and YY is the last two digits of the year.

&SYSDATE is a character string when read into the procedure.

However, if it is not treated as a character string, its use in an expression may result in erroneous results. Since the character string contains slash marks (/), it is interpreted as an arithmetic operation.

In the following SET statements, the user variable &A is set to &SYSDATE and is used in a later SET statement that does not specify it as a character string. Thus, the slash marks in &A are interpreted as arithmetic operators for division. December 25, 1991 is assumed as the current date. The value of &B is computed as 12 divided by 25 divided by 91 giving a result of .0052747.

```
SET &A = &SYSDATE     &A is set to 12/25/91

SET &B = &A           &B is set to ((12/25)/91)
                      which is equal to .0052747
```

The correct usage of the value of &SYSDATE is illustrated in the following SET statements. They treat the variables as a character string by using the system built-in function &STR, thus preventing an arithmetic operation. The &STR function is discussed in the section on system built-in functions.

```
SET &A = &SYSDATE     &A is set to 12/25/91
SET &B = &STR(&A)     &B is set to 12/25/91
```

The current month, day and/or year is selected from &SYSDATE by using a substring. This is the system built-in function &SUBSTR. It is discussed in the section on system functions in this chapter. The statements below read the system clock and set the user variables &MONTH, &DAY and &YEAR to values defined as substrings of the user variable &DATE. Note that the variable &DATE is treated as a character string.

```
SET &DATE = &SYSDATE
SET &MONTH = &SUBSTR(1:2,&STR(&DATE))
SET &DAY = &SUBSTR(4:5,&STR(&DATE))
SET &YEAR = &SUBSTR(7:8,&STR(&DATE))
```

The user variable &DATE is set to the system date. The user variable &MONTH is given a value by selecting the first two characters as a substring from &DATE. Similarly, the value for &DAY is set by extracting a substring of the fourth and fifth characters. The value for &YEAR is set by extracting the seventh and eighth characters as a substring. The slash marks in the third and sixth positions of &DATE are ignored.

&SYSSDATE

The system variable &SYSSDATE also contains the current date from the system clock. However, its format is YY/MM/DD. YY is the last two digits of the year, MM is the two digits for the month and DD is the calendar day in the month.

&SYSSDATE is also an eight-character alphanumeric string and must be specified as a character string the same as &SYSDATE to avoid arithmetic division.

The variable &SYSSDATE is available only in TSO/Extensions.

&SYSJDATE

The variable &SYSJDATE contains the current system date as a six-character alphanumeric character string. Its format is YY.JJJ with YY as the last two digits of the year and JJJ as the relative number of the day in the year. JJJ ranges from 001 for January 1 to 365 for December 31. In leap years, it ranges from 001 to 366.

The variable &SYSJDATE is available only in TSO/Extensions.

&SYSTIME

&SYSTIME contains the current system time. Its value is the eight-character alphanumeric time of the form HH:MM:SS.

The value in &SYSTIME is based on the system's 24 hour clock and the hour ranges from 00 to 24.

&SYSTIME is read from the computer clock as an alphanumeric value. It may be used only as a character string. The same procedures for using substrings to select month, day or year from &SYSDATE may also be used to select the hour, minute or seconds from &SYSTIME.

The following statements extract the hour, minute and second from the current time maintained by the system.

```
SET &TIME = &SYSTIME
SET &HOUR = &SUBSTR(1:2,&STR(&TIME))
SET &MINUTE = &SUBSTR(4:5,&STR(&TIME))
SET &SECOND = &SUBSTR(7:8,&STR(&TIME))
```

&SYSSTIME

&SYSSTIME is the "short" form of the variable &SYSTIME. The format of &SYSSTIME is HH:MM, which presents only the current hour and minutes. Seconds are omitted.

The seconds in &SYSSTIME are truncated. Time is not rounded to the nearest minute. For example, when the system time is 10:30:15, the value of &SYSSTIME is 10:30; however, when the time is 10:30:45, &SYSSTIME will also have the value 10:30.

The value in &SYSSTIME is based on a 24-hour clock where the hour ranges from 00 to 24.

The variable &SYSSTIME is available only in TSO/Extensions.

8.6.2 CPU Utilization

The two system variables &SYSCPU and &SYSSRV contain the CPU time and service units used thus far during the TSO session. This is the time and units accumulated from initial logon to TSO and not from invocation of the CLIST.

CPU time and service units can be very useful during program development and testing to determine the resources used by a program or routine. &SYSCPU and &SYSSRV can also be used to display for the terminal user the amount of CPU time and the service units expended thus far in the TSO session.

These system variables may not be modified.

&SYSCPU

&SYSCPU contains the number of accumulated CPU seconds since the TSO session started. The value of &SYSCPU is the number of CPU seconds and hundredths of seconds.

The format is SS.HH where SS is the number of seconds and HH is hundredths of a second. &SYSCPU is a numeric value that can be used in computations.

In the following example, the CPU time used since logging on to the current TSO session is displayed on the terminal.

```
WRITE The CPU time used in this TSO session is &SYSCPU
```

To determine the number of CPU seconds used for execution of a program, command or other routine, the amount of time from the start to the end of the operation must be computed. The number of CPU seconds at the beginning of the operation must be saved in a user variable. At the completion of the timed operation, this initial CPU time is subtracted from the time at the end of the operation. This is shown in the following example where &SAVETIME is the user variable.

```
SET &SAVETIME = &SYSCPU
CALL 'userid.program.load'
SET &SAVETIME = &SYSCPU - &SAVETIME
WRITE Program execution used &SAVETIME CPU seconds
```

The variable &SYSCPU is available only in TSO/Extensions.

&SYSSRV

&SYSSRV contains a count of the accumulated System Resource Manager (SRM) service units used since logon of the current TSO session. The value of an SRM service unit is defined by the computer facility.

The format is NNNNNNNN where the value is a whole number and &SYSSRV can be used in arithmetic expressions.

The number of service units used by a given program, command or other routine can be determined by subtracting the number of units accumulated at the time an operation began from the number accumulated when the operation ends. The method is the same as shown for determining CPU seconds used in an operation.

The variable &SYSSRV is available only in TSO/Extensions.

8.6.3   Host Environment

There are five system variables that describe the operating environment of the host computer system. They indicate the operational status and level of several operating subsystems on the host computer.

Before executing certain operations in the CLIST, the status and level of required operating subsystems can be determined before the operation is attempted. This may be necessary to avoid operations that may fail if the feature is unavailable or if the CLIST is transferred to other computer systems.

These system variables are available only in TSO/Extensions.

None of the host environment variables may be modified.

&SYSHSM

If the Hierarchical Storage Manager (HSM) is installed, the value of the system variable &SYSHSM is the level of the HSM product. The format of &SYSHSM is VRRM where V is a version number, RR is the release and M is the modification. If the release of HSM is prior to Release 3, &SYSHSM has a value of simply "AVAILABLE".

If HSM is not installed, the value of &SYSHSM is null.

&SYSISPF

The value of &SYSISPF is "ACTIVE" if the ISPF Dialog Manager is operational and "NOT ACTIVE" when it is not available.

&SYSRACF

&SYSRACF indicates the status of the Resource Access Control Facility (RACF), IBM's security subsystem. The value of the &SYSRACF variable is "AVAILABLE" if RACF is installed and is currently operating. The value is "NOT AVAILABLE" when RACF has been installed but is not currently operating. &SYSRACF has a value of "NOT INSTALLED" if RACF is not installed.

&SYSLRACF

&SYSLRACF indicates the version, release and modification of RACF when installed. The format of &SYSRACF is VRRM where V is the version, RR is the release and M is the modification.

If RACF is not installed, the value of &SYSLRACF is null.

&SYSTSOE

The variable &SYSTSOE specifies the version number, release and modification of TSO/E in which the CLIST is executing.

The format of &SYSTSOE is VRRM where V is the version, RR is the release and M is the modification.

8.6.4   Terminal and User

There are five system variables that store information about the user, the TSO session and the terminal being used. This information specifies the user identification (their userID) and the prefix used as the high-level qualifier for dataset names when not fully qualified. The variables also identify the name of the logon procedure executed for the current TSO session. Two of these variables specify the characteristics for the terminal being used for this session, but apply only when TSO Session Manager is in effect.

&SYSUID

&SYSUID contains the user logon identifier or userid. It is retained in the user's profile and cannot be changed.

The value of &SYSUID is one to seven characters depending on computer facility standards for users' TSO identifiers.

The &SYSUID variable may be tested to determine the identity of the user who is executing the CLIST for security or other purposes. Since the user cannot change either his userid or the variable &SYSUID, testing this system variable enables a check on the authority of the user. However, if the user is able to copy or modify the CLIST, any test on &SYSUID can be easily avoided by the user.

&SYSPREF

&SYSPREF contains the prefix used by the system for dataset names. A dataset name is fully qualified when enclosed in single quote marks and will be accepted as is by the system. If not enclosed in quotes, the system prefixes the dataset name with the prefix stored in the user's profile to form a fully qualified name. Upon logon to TSO, the prefix is the same as the userid, but it may be modified by the TSO command PROFILE either in TSO mode or within the CLIST.

The value of &SYSPREF is one to seven characters and depends on facility standards for dataset names.

The value of &SYSPREF may be modified any number of times by issuing the TSO command PROFILE with the PREFIX operand.

The &SYSPREF variable is used when the prefix for a dataset name is not the same as the user's logon identifier. In the example following, the default prefix for dataset names in the user's profile is reset to "SYSTEM1". This modified prefix may be used to identify datasets with high-level qualifiers that are not the same as the user's TSO identifier.

```
PROFILE PREFIX(SYSTEM1)
ALLOCATE FI(ddname) DA('&SYSPREF.name.type')
```

&SYSPROC

&SYSPROC contains the name of the logon procedure used when the user signed on to the current TSO session. The value of &SYSPROC is either the name of the default procedure for the user or the name of the procedure designated by the user for the PROC operand of the LOGON command.

The value of &SYSPROC may not be modified.

&SYSLTERM

The variable &SYSLTERM specifies the number of lines or rows on the user's terminal. It can be reset to alter the number of lines displayed.

&SYSLTERM is available only in TSO/Extensions. Moreover, it can be executed only when Session Manager is in use.

&SYSWTERM

The variable &SYSWTERM specifies the number of characters or columns on each line on the user's terminal. It is reset to change the number of columns displayed.

&SYSWTERM is available only under TSO/Extensions. It can be executed only when Session Manager is in use.

8.6.5   CLIST Execution

There are twelve system variables that can be used to manage certain operational characteristics for executing the CLIST, to test return codes, to temporarily access output generated by TSO commands and subcommands, and to determine the current environment in which the CLIST is executing.

&LASTCC

The computer system issues a condition or return code when a TSO command, subcommand, CLIST statement or other routine is completed. This condition code contains a value to indicate the status of the completed operation. It may indicate that the operation was successful (usually a code of 0) or failed due to some condition (usually a code greater than 0). Some user programs also issue return codes to indicate the status of the operation.

&LASTCC contains the condition or return code issued by the last statement executed. The value in &LASTCC may be tested to determine the success or failure of the operation.

Condition codes, which can be issued by a system program or a utility, by a user program, by any TSO command or subcommand, or by any CLIST statement, can have a value ranging from 0 to 4095. Therefore, the minimum value of &LASTCC is 0 while the maximum value is 4095. Condition codes must be positive whole numbers.

The following are examples of using &LASTCC.

```
WRITE The condition code from program XYZ is &LASTCC
IF &LASTCC > 4, THEN WRITE Program failed with &LASTCC
```

When any statement is executed after an operation whose code is to be tested, its condition code replaces the prior value of &LASTCC. Therefore, any condition code to be tested must be immediately saved in a user variable. The examples below demonstrate that a condition code must be immediately stored in a user variable if it is to be used in a later statement.

The example below allocates an online file and then executes a test of &LASTCC to determine if the allocation succeeded. The following code assumes that the file allocation was not successful and the system issued a condition code of 4. The values of &LASTCC on the right are issued upon completion of each statement. Even though the code issued by the ALLOCATE statement is 4, the test IF &LASTCC > 0 is false because the preceding statement IF LASTCC = 0 issued a return code of 0. Thus, the conditional branch to LABEL2 cannot be executed.

```
ALLOCATE FI(INPUT) DA(MYFILE.DATA) OLD     &LASTCC = 4
IF &LASTCC = 0, THEN GOTO LABEL1           &LASTCC = 0
```

```
IF &LASTCC > 0, THEN GOTO LABEL2        &LASTCC = 0
GOTO LABEL3                             &LASTCC = 0
```

The above example is changed below to store the value of the &LASTCC variable in the user variable &RETNCD for subsequent testing. This modification will ensure the retention of the actual code returned by the ALLOCATE command. The branch to LABEL2 will be executed since the value of &LASTCC issued by the ALLOCATE command was saved.

```
ALLOCATE FI(INPUT) DA(MYFILE.DATA) OLD   &LASTCC = 4
SET &RETNCD = &LASTCC                    &LASTCC = 0
                                        &RETNCD = 4
IF &RETNCD = 0, THEN GOTO LABEL1         &LASTCC = 0
                                        &RETNCD = 4
IF &RETNCD > 0, THEN GOTO LABEL2         &LASTCC = 0
                                        &RETNCD = 4
GOTO LABEL3                             &LASTCC = 0
                                        &RETNCD = 4
```

&MAXCC

&MAXCC is the highest condition or return code issued by any of the commands or statements executed thus far in the CLIST procedure. This system variable is most frequently used to terminate CLIST processing or to perform alternate or remedial action when any earlier statements or programs have issued a condition code equal to or greater than a desired number.

A condition code issued by any program, command or statement must be from 0 to 4095. Thus, the minimum &MAXCC value is 0 and its maximum value is 4095. Condition codes may not be a negative value and must be whole numbers.

The following example demonstrates one use of &MAXCC. This test of the value of &MAXCC is true because the TSO ALLOCATE command issued a condition code of 8. Therefore, the branch to ERRORS will be executed.

```
ALLOCATE FI(INPUT) DA(MYFILE.DATA) OLD   &LASTCC = 8
                                        &MAXCC  = 8
```

```
ALLOCATE FI(PRICE) DA(PRICES.DATA) NEW       &LASTCC = 0
                                             &MAXCC  = 8
ALLOCATE FI(INFIL) DA(INFILE.DATA) OLD       &LASTCC = 4
                                             &MAXCC  = 8
IF &MAXCC > 4, THEN GOTO ERRORS              &LASTCC = 0
                                             &MAXCC  = 8
```

Note that &MAXCC retains the highest code returned by any of the operations performed, but does not indicate which of the operations issued the condition code. If it is necessary to retain the return codes issued by specific operations, they can be saved by storing &LASTCC in different user variables.

&SYSDVAL

&SYSDVAL contains the responses from a terminal user either when a READ statement with no operands is executed or when a TERMIN statement is executed and control is returned to the CLIST.

A READ statement accepts input from a terminal user. It may have a user-specified variable as an operand to receive the response as shown below. A WRITE or WRITENR statement should precede the READ statement to indicate what kind of response the user is expected to give.

```
WRITE ENTER THE THREE-CHARACTER NAME OF THE MONTH
READ &MONTH
```

In this example, if the user responds with "DEC", the value of the user variable &MONTH will be DEC.

Alternatively, the READ statement may not specify an operand, and the user's response is stored in the &SYSDVAL variable.

```
WRITE ENTER THE THREE-CHARACTER NAME OF THE MONTH
READ
```

In this example, no operand was specified for READ. If the user responds with "DEC", the value in &SYSDVAL will be DEC.

&SYSDVAL can be used in subsequent operations such as IF and SET statements. Note that the value in &SYSDVAL is modified upon the next READ or TERMIN statement executed.

A TERMIN statement transfers operating control to a terminal user. The statement specifies one or more character strings from which the user can choose to return operating control. This character string is referred to as a delimiter. It is immediately followed by the user's response, which is stored in the system variable &SYSDVAL.

In the example below, the CLIST presents two options for the user to enter a delimiter as well as a name of a month. The user responds with the second delimiter and with a value of "DEC" to answer the request for a month name.

```
WRITE ENTER THE THREE-CHARACTER NAME OF THE MONTH
WRITE AFTER THE TERM "STOP" OR "DONE"
TERMIN STOP DONE
     user response is DONE DEC
     value of &SYSDLM is 2
     value of &SYSDVAL is DEC
SET &MONTH = &SYSDVAL
IF &SYSDLM = 2, THEN GOTO LABEL2
```

&SYSDLM

&SYSDLM contains the value of the positional number of the delimiter string entered by the terminal user in response to a TERMIN statement. When the TERMIN statement is executed, control is passed to the user. The user returns control to the CLIST by entering one of the character strings specified on the TERMIN statement. More than one character string can be specified on the TERMIN statement, and the user can answer with any one of them. The value of &SYSDLM is the numerical relative position of the character string chosen by the user when control is returned to the CLIST.

The value of &SYSDLM can be used to determine the particular character string selected and to select options based on the user's choice. The following example shows how &SYSDLM can be used to make branching decisions.

```
WRITE WHEN FINISHED, ENTER "STOP" IF COMPLETED OR
WRITE    ENTER "MORE" IF THERE ARE MORE TASKS
TERMIN STOP MORE
     . . . . .
     user activity
     . . . . .
     user response when finished is MORE
IF &SYSDLM = 1, THEN GOTO LABEL1
IF &SYSDLM = 2, THEN GOTO LABEL2
```

The value of &SYSDLM in this example is 2 since the terminal user responded with the term "MORE", the term in the second position of the TERMIN statement. If the user had responded with "STOP", the value of &SYSDLM would be 1.

&SYSSCAN

&SYSSCAN contains a numeric value that specifies the maximum number of times a statement is to be scanned to resolve its symbolic variables. The default value is 16. This variable can be modified by the user to any value from 0 to 2**31 by the SET statement as shown below.

```
SET &SYSSCAN = number
```

When the value of &SYSSCAN is set to 0, no scan is performed and symbolic variables in statements executed after &SYSSCAN is set equal to 0 are not resolved. Resolution of variables resumes after &SYSSCAN is reset to any value greater than 0.

&SYSOUTTRAP

The system variable &SYSOUTTRAP specifies the maximum number of lines of terminal display generated by execution of a TSO command or subcommand. Most of the commands and subcommands generate one or more lines of information and often include the result of the operation. Usually, these lines are displayed at the user's terminal and cannot be subsequently accessed.

&SYSOUTTRAP may be set to any positive number to specify

the maximum number of display lines to be "trapped," or saved.

When &SYSOUTTRAP is set to 0, no lines are saved. If output is to be saved, &SYSOUTTRAP should be reset to 0 immediately after the command to be trapped is executed. If &SYSOUTTRAP is not reset, the output generated by a subsequent statement will overlay the lines saved earlier.

When more lines are generated than the number designated for &SYSOUTTRAP, the excess lines are not saved.

A count of the lines generated by executing a TSO command or subcommand is stored in the system variable &SYSOUTLINE.

Trapped output is retrieved by the &SYSOUTLINEnn variable.

An example of using &SYSOUTTRAP is offered in the discussion on the variables &SYSOUTLINE and &SYSOUTLINEnn.

&SYSOUTLINE and &SYSOUTLINEnn

When output is generated by a TSO command or subcommand, the system saves the count of lines in the system variable named &SYSOUTLINE. The value in &SYSOUTLINE is thus the number of lines produced.

Trapped output can be accessed only on a line-by-line basis. When output lines are generated, provided &SYSOUTTRAP is set to a number more than 0, they are stored in system variables named &SYSOUTLINEnn. The number "nn" in the variable's name is a relative number starting with 1. The first output line is recorded in &SYSOUTLINE1, the second line in &SYSOUTLINE2 and so forth. The number "nn" may be any positive number up to 21 digits in length.

The following example illustrates using the system variables &SYSOUTTRAP, &SYSOUTLINE and &SYSOUTLINEnn. In the example, a dataset named PAYROLL.DATA contains 500 records or lines. However, the limit for &SYSOUTTRAP is set to 100. Moreover, the TSO command LIST also lists the dataset name that will be trapped as the first line. Thus, only 99 records can be saved; they are stored in the variables &SYSOUTLINE2 through &SYSOUTLINE100. Also, the last statement in the coding sets a user variable named &RECD25 to the value in &SYSOUTLINE26. The 26th line in the output is the 25th record from the dataset since the output has a dataset name as the first line.

```
SET &SYSOUTTRAP = 100
LIST PAYROLL.DATA
IF &LASTCC > 0, THEN EXIT      /* Error in dataset */
IF &SYSOUTLINE = 1, THEN EXIT  /* Data set is empty */
SET &RECD25 = &SYSOUTLINE26    /* Reads 25th record */
```

This example illustrates the necessity of knowing the number and the format of output lines generated by TSO commands and subcommands when their output is to be stored by &SYSOUTTRAP and retrieved by &SYSOUTLINE and &SYSOUTLINEnn.

&SYSENV

&SYSENV has a value of either FORE or BACK to indicate that the CLIST is executing in the system foreground in TSO or in the system background as a batch job.

Knowing whether the CLIST is executing in interactive TSO or in a batch job may be critical to its success. For example, the terminal user can be prompted for additional information when a TSO command or subcommand is executed. Of course, in the batch job environment, this is not possible.

However, responses that a user might enter could be included as input data in the batch job when the values of that input are known in advance. The CLIST could include the statement DATA PROMPT .... ENDDATA to enclose the anticipated input to the system prompt.

The following example illustrates the use of &SYSENV as well as actions that can be taken when the CLIST may be executed in either foreground or background processing.

```
CHECK: IF &SYSENV = FORE, THEN GOTO INTER
       IF &SYSENV = BACK, THEN GOTO BATCH
INTER: COPY A.DATA
       system prompts user for name of output dataset
       GOTO .....
BATCH: COPY A.DATA
       DATA PROMPT
       b.data
       ENDDATA
       GOTO .....
```

&SYSICMD

&SYSICMD contains the name of the CLIST being executed if it is implicitly invoked as a member of a partitioned dataset. The value of &SYSICMD is null if it was explicitly invoked.

```
EXEC (MYPROC)      (Explicit)      &SYSICMD = null

MYPROC             (Implicit)      &SYSICMD = MYPROC
```

&SYSPCMD

&SYSPCMD contains the name of the most recently executed TSO command in the CLIST. Its initial value is EXEC when in the command environment and is the name of the TSO command, such as EDIT or TEST, when in the subcommand environment. In the following example, the value of &SYSPCMD did not change when the SET and WRITE statements were executed since the name of the last TSO command executed is always used as the value.

```
PROC 0                            &SYSPCMD = EXEC
SET &A = 100                      &SYSPCMD = EXEC
ALLOC FI(X) DA(X.DATA)            &SYSPCMD = ALLOC
WRITE EDIT OF X.DATA BEGINNING    &SYSPCMD = ALLOC
EDIT X.DATA                       &SYSPCMD = EDIT
CHANGE 0030 /1/2/                 &SYSPCMD = EDIT
END SAVE                          &SYSPCMD = EDIT
FREE FI(X)                        &SYSPCMD = FREE
```

&SYSSCMD

&SYSSCMD contains the name of the subcommand currently being executed. If, for example, EDIT is executed in a CLIST, the names of the EDIT subcommands are stored in &SYSSCMD as they are executed. The value of &SYSSCMD is null if a subcommand is not being executed.

```
PROC 0                            &SYSSCMD = null
WRITE EDIT OF X.DATA BEGINNING    &SYSSCMD = null
EDIT X.DATA                       &SYSSCMD = null
```

```
FIND /ABC/                        &SYSSCMD = FIND
DOWN                              &SYSSCMD = DOWN
CHANGE * 30 /1/2/                 &SYSSCMD = CHANGE
END SAVE                          &SYSSCMD = END
FREE FI(X)                        &SYSSCMD = null
```

&SYSNEST

&SYSNEST contains the value YES if the CLIST currently being executed is a nested CLIST, and NO if it is not nested.

```
PROC 0                            &SYSNEST = NO
SET &A = 100                      &SYSNEST = NO
EXEC NESTPROC '&A'                &SYSNEST = YES
        .....                     &SYSNEST = YES
        EXIT                      &SYSNEST = YES
SET &B = &A * 2                   &SYSNEST = NO
```

8.6.6   CONTROL Command Values

There are seven system variables that enable the capability to test and/or to reset the status of the various options on the CLIST statement CONTROL. The CONTROL statement and its functions are discussed in Chapter 9.

Briefly, the CONTROL statement defines certain options that can be in effect during CLIST execution. The CLIST may have any number of CONTROL statements to turn these options on or off.

An alternative to executing subsequent CONTROL statements is to use these system variables to define CONTROL options.

The purpose of each of these seven variables is given below. A review of the CONTROL statement is suggested to completely comprehend the purpose of each of these system variables.

Each of these Control Command variables may have a value of only ON or OFF. The status of the Control option must be reset by a SET statement that assigns an ON or OFF value to the system variable. The following examples illustrate changing the status of the variable &SYSMSG.

```
SET &SYSMSG = ON
SET &SYSMSG = OFF
```

The current value of any Control option can be determined by executing an IF test on the variable. In the following example, the current status of the CONTROL statement operand MSG that enables the display of system error and information messages is tested by an IF condition.

```
IF &SYSMSG = ON, THEN .....
IF &SYSMSG = OFF, THEN .....
```

All of these Control Command variables are available only in TSO/Extensions.

&SYSASIS

When &SYSASIS is OFF, the CAPS option is in effect and lower-case letters are translated to upper case. When &SYSASIS is ON, the ASIS option is in effect and lowercase letters will not be converted.

&SYSFLUSH

When &SYSFLUSH is OFF, the NOFLUSH option is in effect. The CLIST is not flushed (ended) if an error or interrupt occurs during execution. When &SYSFLUSH is ON, the FLUSH option is in effect and the CLIST can be flushed if an interrupt or an error occurs.

&SYSMSG

When &SYSMSG is OFF, the NOMSG option is in effect. System informational and error messages are suppressed. If &SYSMSG is ON, system informational and error messages are displayed on the terminal.

&SYSPROMPT

When &SYSPROMPT is OFF, the NOPROMPT option is in effect, and TSO commands or subcommands are inhibited from prompting the terminal user. When &SYSPROMPT is ON, the PROMPT option is in effect, and the system can prompt the user.

&SYSLIST

When &SYSLIST is OFF, the NOLIST option is in effect, and TSO commands and subcommands are not listed at the terminal. If &SYSLIST is ON, the LIST option is in effect, and commands or subcommands are listed as they are executed.

&SYSCONLIST

If &SYSCONLIST is OFF, the NOCONLIST option is in effect, and CLIST statements are not listed. When &SYSPROMPT is ON, the CONLIST option is in effect, and CLIST statements are listed as they are executed after symbolic substitution.

&SYSSYMLIST

If &SYSSYMLIST is OFF, the NOSYMLIST option is in effect, and executable statements (CLIST commands, TSO commands/ subcommands) are not displayed. When &SYSSYMLIST is ON, executable statements are listed at the terminal, before symbolic substitution, as they are executed.

8.6.7   Dataset Information

There are twenty-five Dataset Information system variables. They contain information on the attributes of an online dataset. These attributes describe its physical characteristics and allocation information. Examples of attributes are dataset name, logical record length, physical block size, create date, security status, and disk space allocated and used.

The values for the Dataset Information system variables are set when the CLIST statement LISTDSI is executed, and contain the attributes for the dataset specified for the statement.

The following demonstrates the use of the LISTDSI statement. After LISTDSI is executed, the attributes of dataset X.DATA are saved in the Dataset Information system variables. The LISTDSI statement is discussed in Chapter 9.

```
LISTDSI X.DATA
```

When an item of attribute information is missing or invalid, the value of its associated variable is filled with a series of question marks (?). When the dataset is a VSAM index or data component or other VSAM file, only &SYSVOLUME, &SYSUNIT and &SYSDSORG can be determined. All other variables have a value of question marks.

All of the Dataset Information variables are available only in TSO/Extensions.

Dataset Name

&SYSDSNAME   — Name of the dataset

Device Specifications

&SYSUNIT   — Type of device where the dataset resides

&SYSVOLUME   — Serial identifier of the volume where the dataset resides

&SYSTRKSCYL   — Tracks per cylinder for device type

&SYSBLKSTRK   — Directory blocks per track for device type

Dataset Security

&SYSPASSWORD   — Status of IBM OS password protection

&SYSRACFA   — Status of IBM RACF security

Dataset Physical Characteristics

&SYSDSORG   — Dataset organization
&SYSRECFM   — Record format
&SYSLRECL   — Logical record length
&SYSBLKSIZE   — Physical block size
&SYSKEYLEN   — Key length for variable length records

Disk Space Allocation

&SYSALLOC   — Total disk space allocated
&SYSUSED   — Total disk space used
&SYSPRIMARY   — Primary (initial) disk space specification
&SYSSECONDS   — Secondary disk space specification

| &SYSUNITS | — Units (cylinders, tracks, blocks) of space allocation |
| &SYSEXTENTS | — Number of physical extents occupied |

Creation, Expiration and Reference Dates

&SYSCREATE	— Creation date in yyyy/ddd format
&SYSEXDATE	— Expiration date in yyyy/ddd format
&SYSREFDATE	— Last reference date in yyyy/ddd format
&SYSUPDATED	— YES if dataset updated and NO if not

PDS Directories and Members

&SYSADIRBLK	— Number of allocated PDS directory blocks
&SYSUDIRBLK	— Number of PDS directory blocks used
&SYSMEMBERS	— Number of members in PDS

8.7   SYSTEM BUILT-IN FUNCTIONS

There are eleven system built-in functions. They are system-defined symbolic variables. Their values are the product of evaluating an associated expression. The format of a system built-in function is shown below. The variable name for the function is titled "&function" and the associated expression is the term "expression" enclosed in parentheses. There are no spaces or other delimiters between the function name and the opening parenthesis.

```
&function(expression)
```

The expression may be a simple character string or numerical value or it may be a complex expression containing variables to be resolved, character strings and arithmetic operations. The expression can include nested expressions.

&SYSDSN

The function &SYSDSN is used to determine if a disk dataset or a PDS member exists. The values of &SYSDSN depend on the type and status of the dataset, and whether any errors were encountered in processing the statement. The values are:

```
OK
MEMBER SPECIFIED BUT DATASET IS NOT PARTITIONED
MEMBER NOT FOUND
DATASET NOT FOUND
ERROR PROCESSING REQUESTED DATASET
PROTECTED DATASET
VOLUME NOT ON SYSTEM
UNAVAILABLE DATASET
INVALID DATASET NAME
MISSING DATASET NAME
```

In the following example, the PDS named ABC.DATA has members named X, Y and Z. The value of &SYSDSN is on the right.

```
&SYSDSN(ABC.DATA)          OK
&SYSDSN(ABC.DATA(A))       MEMBER NOT FOUND
&SYSDSN(ABC.DATA(Z))       OK
```

&DATATYPE

&DATATYPE contains the value NUM if the evaluated expression is wholly numeric, whereas it contains the value CHAR if the expression includes any non-numeric characters. &DATATYPE is used to determine if an item is numeric or non-numeric.

In the following examples, it is assumed that the value in user variable &A is 12345 and the value in &B is ABC. The values of the system function &DATATYPE are shown on the right.

```
&DATATYPE(123D5)       CHAR
&DATATYPE(67890)       NUM
&DATATYPE(&A)          NUM
&DATATYPE(&B)          CHAR
```

```
&DATATYPE((&A*10)/5)              NUM
&DATATYPE(&A&B)                   CHAR
```

The following example demonstrates one very important use of the system function &DATATYPE. Testing the variable &AMOUNT to confirm that it is numeric avoids an erroneous result and abnormal termination of the procedure. Moreover, it enables selecting a path to take depending on whether the value is numeric or non-numeric.

```
GETAMT: WRITE Enter a Numeric Amount
REREAD: READ &AMOUNT
        IF &DATATYPE(&AMOUNT) = NUM, THEN GOTO ADDAMT
        WRITE Amount is Not Numeric - Please Re-Enter
        GOTO REREAD
ADDAMT: SET &TOTAL = &TOTAL + &AMOUNT
```

&SYSCAPS

&SYSCAPS converts letters in the associated character string or expression to upper case. It does not change any numbers or special characters. In the following examples, the value of the user variable &A is ABc123deF%g. The resultant value contained in &SYSCAPS is shown on the right.

```
&SYSCAPS(ABCDE)                   ABCDE
&SYSCAPS(xyz)                     XYZ
&SYSCAPS(&A)                      ABC123DEF%G
```

&SYSLC

&SYSLC converts letters in an associated character string or expression to lower case. It does not change any numbers or special characters. In the examples below, the value of the user variable &A is ABc123deF%g. &SYSLC values are given in the right column.

```
&SYSLC(ABCDE)                     abcde
&SYSLC(xyz)                       xyz
&SYSLC(&A)                        abc123def%g
```

&EVAL

&EVAL contains the calculated value of a numeric expression. The terms in the expression are resolved and then arithmetic operations are performed. The result is stored as the value of &EVAL. This function may be performed only on expressions having all terms and variables with numeric values.

In the following examples, the variable &A has a value of 50 and &B has a value of 25. The computed value of &EVAL is on the right.

```
&EVAL((12 / (2 + 2)            3
&EVAL(&A + &B)                75
&EVAL((&A - 10) + (&B * 2))    90
```

Arithmetic expressions in CLIST statements WRITE and WRITENR are not evaluated. WRITE and WRITENR send text for terminal display. These statements are presented in Chapter 9.

In order to resolve an arithmetic expression in a WRITE or a WRITENR statement, the system function &EVAL resolves all of the variables in the expression and performs the arithmetic.

For example, the following statement does not include &EVAL. It does not display the desired message.

```
WRITE The product of 3 times 5 is 3*5
Display:  The product of 3 times 5 is 3*5
```

The statement above is modified to include &EVAL(3*5). This performs the arithmetic and displays the desired message.

```
WRITE The product of 3 times 5 is &EVAL(3*5)
Display:  The product of 3 times 5 is 15
```

&LENGTH

&LENGTH contains a numeric value that is equal to the length of the result of evaluating an associated expression.

All of the variables in the expression are resolved and then arithmetic operations are performed. The result is examined and a count of the number of characters is made. The number of characters is the length of that result of evaluating the associated expression.

Therefore, &LENGTH is a count of the number of characters or digits in the result of an expression when all variables are resolved and all arithmetic operations are performed.

In the following examples, it is assumed that the user variable &A has a value of 100, &B has the value 5 and &C has a value of ABCDEF. The result of evaluating the expression is given, and the value of &LENGTH is shown.

```
                                 Result        Length

&LENGTH(&A)                         100           3
&LENGTH(&A / &B)                     20           2
&LENGTH((&A * 10) - &B)             995           3
&LENGTH(&STR(ABCD))                ABCD           4
&LENGTH(&STR(&C))                ABCDEF           6
&LENGTH(&SUBSTR(2:3,&C))             BC           2
```

The &LENGTH function is often used for determining whether a variable has any value or is null. The number of characters in a null value is zero. In all other instances, &LENGTH is greater than zero. In the first example below, the value of &A is null, &LENGTH is zero and the branch to LABEL1 occurs. In the second example, the value of &A is not null, &LENGTH is 2 and the branch is not executed.

```
SET &A =
IF &LENGTH(&A) = 0, THEN GOTO LABEL1

SET &A = 50
IF &LENGTH(&A) = 0, THEN GOTO LABEL1
```

&STR

&STR prevents arithmetic computation of a numeric expression but performs substitution of variables and nested functions. It is used to maintain a character string that includes any arithmetic operators, numbers or delimiters (spaces, commas) as a set of valid alphanumeric characters without performing any arithmetic operations. The terms and values in the &STR expression may be one or any number of operators, variables, characters and nested functions.

System or user variables often contain operators and numeric values that are not intended for arithmetic operation. The system function &SYSDATE is a good example since it includes slash marks that are interpreted as division operators. The &STR function inhibits arithmetic operations and retains the date value in the format MM/DD/YY.

The following examples demonstrate the use of the &STR function. It is assumed that the value for &A is 5 and &B is DECEMBER. The value of &STR after its expression is resolved is listed on the right.

```
&STR(&A)                   5
&STR(10+&A)                10+5
&STR(10 + &A)              10 + 5
&STR(00.&A)                00.5
&STR(&B.91)                DECEMBER91
&STR(&B 25, 1991)          DECEMBER 25, 1991
&STR(&SYSDATE)             12/25/91
&STR(12/25/91)             12/25/91
```

In each of these examples, every variable has been resolved. However, no arithmetic operations were performed even though the second and third examples include a plus sign within the expression. In the last two examples, a slash mark normally denoting division is included in the expression. In each of these examples, the arithmetic operator is treated simply as another alphanumeric character.

The CLIST interpreter drops leading zeros in numeric values. When leading zeros are required, the value should be treated as a &STR function. The following examples present the use of &STR to retain leading zeros. The values of &A are given on the right.

```
SET &A = 100 / 5           20
SET &A = &STR(00&A)        0020

SET &A = 5 / 100           .05
SET &A = &STR(0&A)         0.05
```

&NRSTR

The function &NRSTR prevents deletion of the first ampersand in an item prefixed with double ampersands. When an item is examined, it is assumed to be a variable name when it begins with an ampersand. The leading ampersand is removed and the variable is resolved.

However, temporary dataset names on IBM systems have double ampersands (&&) as a prefix. When a temporary dataset name is referred to in a CLIST, the CLIST interpreter assumes the name is a variable name and removes the first ampersand, with the result no longer being the name of a temporary dataset.

This problem is avoided by always referring to the temporary name with the &NRSTR function as shown in the following example. The value of &NRSTR is given on the right.

```
SET &DSN = &&X          &X          (Variable name)
SET &DSN = &NRSTR(&&X)   &&X         (Temporary name)
```

&SYSNSUB

The system function &SYSNSUB limits the number of times that symbolic substitution is performed to resolve a variable.

Defining the number of times that the variable is scanned to resolve it can be used to override rules for ampersands that prefix variable names and that identify temporary datasets.

The expression associated with &SYSNSUB must include a whole number from 0 to 99 to set the number of times that symbolic substitution is to be performed. When the value is 0, there is no symbolic substitution.

The format of &SYSNSUB is shown here. "n" is the number of times substitution is to be performed. The value of "n" may not exceed a limit established by the &SYSSCAN variable.

```
&SYSNSUB(n,expression)
```

Note that &SYSNSUB limits symbolic substitution for a single term or expression while the system variable &SYSSCAN limits symbolic substitution, in general, for every expression. Scan limits set by &SYSSCAN can, of course, be reset by executing another SET &SYSSCAN statement.

&SUBSTR

&SUBSTR contains a range of consecutive characters extracted from a parent character string. The selection of characters from the parent string is based on identifying the first and last positions of the substring to be extracted. The number of characters that may be extracted is one or any number up to the total length of the parent string.

The values that specify the first and last positions in the substring must be numeric and must be separated by a colon.

The value to specify the first position must be less than or equal to the value specifying the last position. Either or both positions may also be variables or expressions, provided that the result of resolving the variable or expression will be a whole number.

The range is closed with a comma and followed by the string. The complete expression, consisting of both the range and the string, is enclosed in parentheses.

```
&SUBSTR(first:last,string)
```

The following examples present the use of the &SUBSTR function. The positions expressed as whole numbers or as calculated by evaluating an expression are shown in the indicated columns. The extracted substrings are listed on the right. In these examples, the value of &A is 2, &B is 4 and &X = ABCDEF.

	First	Last	Substring
&SUBSTR(2:5,&X)	2	5	BCDE
&SUBSTR(2:&B,&X)	2	4	BCD
&SUBSTR(&A:&A,&STR(67890))	2	2	7
&SUBSTR(&A:(&A+&B-2),67890)	2	4	789
&SUBSTR(&B:4,&STR(123+45)	4	4	+
&SUBSTR(1:2,&SYSDATE)	1	2	12
&SUBSTR(&B:5,&STR(12/25/91))	4	5	25

If a single character is to be extracted, only that position must be specified. Alternatively, a first and last position may be specified provided they are the same. This syntax is illustrated here.

	First	Last	Substring
&SUBSTR(3,&X)	3	3	C
&SUBSTR(3:3,&X)	3	3	C

&SYSINDEX

The function &SYSINDEX determines the starting position of a character string within another character string. &SYSINDEX can be used to find out if a character string contains a set of one or more characters and, if so, where those characters are located in the string.

The value of &SYSINDEX is a number indicating the beginning position of the embedded character string. If the character string is not included within the other string, the value of &SYSINDEX will be 0.

Either or both of the character strings could be literals or expressions.

Optionally, a whole number may be specified to designate the starting position in which to begin a search. If the option is not included, the search begins in the first position.

The format of &SYSINDEX is shown here. "string1" specifies the string to be located, "string2" identifies the string in which to search, and "n" is an optional starting position to begin the search.

```
&SYSINDEX(string1,string2,n)
```

The following examples show how the &SYSINDEX function might be used to determine if a string is contained within another string and, if it is, where it is located. Note that either string argument may be a literal or an expression. These examples assume that a user variable &A has a value of "CLIST", user variable &B has the value "LANGUAGE", and user variable &N has a numeric value 5. The result of evaluating each expression is shown to the right of the example.

```
&SYSINDEX(CD,ABCDEF)        3
&SYSINDEX(L,&A)             2
&SYSINDEX(L,&A,3)           0
&SYSINDEX(&A,&B)            0
&SYSINDEX(A,&B)             2
```

```
&SYSINDEX(A,&B,&N)                6
&SYSINDEX((&SUBSTR(2,&A)),&B)     1
```

8.8   EXERCISES

1. Match the types of variables listed below with the one or more statements that describe them. Some statements will describe more than one type of variable.

a. Positional parameter   **e.** Dataset input/output
b. Keyword parameter   **f.** Terminal input
c. System-defined   **g.** User-defined
d. Built-in function   **h.** Global

_____ Defined in a PROC statement

_____ Value is determined by evaluating an associated expression

_____ Defined by the CLIST writer

_____ Receives data from an end user

_____ Determines whether a variable is alphanumeric or numeric

_____ Contains the contents of one dataset record

_____ Passes values to nested CLISTs

_____ May not be modified in the CLIST

_____ Must be defined and read in positional order

_____ May be assigned a default value

_____ Values are set initially by a terminal user when the CLIST is initiated

_____ Variable name must be identical to the name specified in a TSO command

_____ Automatically available in all levels of nested CLISTs

_____ May be initially defined in different kinds of CLIST statements

2. Determine the results of evaluating each of the following expressions. The values of the variables are:

&A = ABC   &B = 120   &C = A2C   &D = 10
&E = e   &F =   &G = 1   &H = 2

Also, assume the current system date is July 4, 1992, the time is 3:30:45 PM and the variable &DATE is equal to the system variable &SYSDATE.

```
&SYSDATE                                          _____

&SYSTIME                                          _____

&DATATYPE(&C)                                     _____

&DATATYPE(&DATE)                                  _____

&DATATYPE(&STR(&DATE))                            _____

&SYSCAPS(&A&E)                                    _____

&SYSLC(&A&STR(&SYSSTIME))                         _____

&EVAL(125/(&D/&H))                                _____

&EVAL((&B+&C+&D)/5)                               _____

&LENGTH(&F)                                       _____

&LENGTH(&SUBSTR(&G,&A))                           _____

&SUBSTR(&G:(&D/&H),&STR(&DATE))                   _____

&SUBSTR(&G:(&D/&H),&DATE)                         _____

&SYSINDEX(C,&A)                                   _____

&SYSINDEX(A,&C,&H)                                _____

&B + &D / &H                                      _____

(&B + &D) / &H                                    _____

((&G ** &H) - 1)                                  _____
```

3. Evaluate each of the IF statements below and determine if the condition is true or false. The variables are set to the following values.

&A = ABC   &B = 120   &C = A2C   &D = 10
&E = e   &F =   &G = 1   &H = 2

Also, assume that the current system date is July 4, 1992 and the current time is 3:30 PM.

```
IF &A LE &C                                          _____

IF &A EQ &C                                          _____

IF &B NE (&B * &G)                                   _____

IF &G = &LENGTH(&E)                                  _____

IF &H GT &LENGTH(&B / &D)                            _____

IF &H < &SUBSTR(4:&D/&H,&STR(&SYSDATE))              _____

IF &DATATYPE(&E) EQ NUM OR +
   &LENGTH(&D) EQ &H                                 _____

IF &LENGTH(&C) GT &H AND +
   &D LT &H                                          _____
```

9

CLIST Statements

A CLIST is a command procedure that consists of one or more CLIST statements. It may also include any TSO commands and subcommands. CLIST statements are the commands of the CLIST language. They perform many functions: define variables and assign values to them; execute branches, conditional actions and loops; perform input/output to a terminal or a file; and execute comparative, logical and arithmetic operations.

9.1 TABLE OF CLIST STATEMENT FUNCTIONS

There are 32 commands (statements) in the CLIST language and nine categories of functional capabilities. Every statement is listed below in its primary functional capability. Their general format and operands are also illustrated.

Two of these, EXEC and WHEN SYSRC, are not CLIST statements. Instead, they are TSO commands. However, they are included since they directly relate to and are often used in CLISTs.

Manage the Operating Environment

```
CONTROL operands
DATA ..... ENDDATA
DATA PROMPT ..... ENDDATA
TERMIN , strings
```

Define and Assign Variables

```
SET variable EQ expression
PROC n positionals keywords(value)
GLOBAL variables
NGLOBAL variables
```

Perform Terminal Input/Output

```
WRITE text
WRITENR text
READ variables
READDVAL variables
```

List Dataset Information

```
LISTDSI dsname operands
```

Perform Dataset Input/Output

```
OPENFILE filename mode
GETFILE filename
PUTFILE filename
CLOSFILE filename
```

Establish Conditional Action

```
IF comparison THEN action
              ELSE action
DO ..... END
SELECT expression WHEN (condition) action
                  OTHERWISE action ..... END
```

Control Execution Sequence

```
EXEC dsname parameters
END
EXIT CODE(expression) QUIT
GOTO label
```

Perform CLIST Subprocedures

```
PROC n positionals keywords(value) ..... END
SYSCALL label parameters
SYSREF variables
RETURN CODE(expression)
```

Manage Errors and Interrupts

```
ATTN action
ERROR action
RETURN
WHEN SYSRC(operator integer) action
```

Statements are discussed on the following pages within these categories. For each statement, the following is presented.

Category: Primary functional capability.

Function: Description of statement function and usage.

Format: Statement syntax and format and its operands. Default operands are underlined and optional operands are in brackets as in [operand].

Operands: Description of each operand and its function. Default operands are underlined.

Examples: One or more examples to demonstrate the CLIST statement and its operands.

Notes: Added clarification, special requirements for the statement, references to other statements and other explanatory material as needed.

9.2   CONTROL

Category: Manage the Operating Environment

Function: The CONTROL statement defines certain operational options to be turned on when the CONTROL statement is executed. These options specify characteristics that are to be in effect. Options specified on a CONTROL statement may be cancelled or changed in a subsequent CONTROL statement. One or more CONTROL statements in CLISTs in development and testing are an extremely effective aid in debugging by displaying statements as they are executed.

Format: CONTROL $\begin{bmatrix} \underline{FLUSH} \\ NOFLUSH \end{bmatrix}$ $\begin{bmatrix} PROMPT \\ \underline{NOPROMPT} \end{bmatrix}$ $\begin{bmatrix} LIST \\ \underline{NOLIST} \end{bmatrix}$

$\begin{bmatrix} CONLIST \\ \underline{NOCONLIST} \end{bmatrix}$ $\begin{bmatrix} SYMLIST \\ \underline{NOSYMLIST} \end{bmatrix}$ $\begin{bmatrix} \underline{MSG} \\ NOMSG \end{bmatrix}$

[MAIN] $\begin{bmatrix} \underline{CAPS} \\ ASIS \end{bmatrix}$ [END(string)]

Operands: FLUSH   — Allows the system to flush the stack when an attention interrupt or error condition occurs. See notes below.

NOFLUSH   — Prevents the system from flushing or purging the stack if an interrupt or error condition occurs.

PROMPT   — Enables the CLIST to prompt the user for input. See notes below.

NOPROMPT   — Prevents the command procedure from prompting the user even when the TSO session has prompting capabilities.

LIST   — Displays TSO commands or subcommands at a terminal after substitution for variables but before execution. It does not display CLIST statements.

NOLIST   — Prevents the display of TSO commands and subcommands at the terminal.

CONLIST — Displays CLIST statements at the terminal after symbolic substitution but before execution. It does not display TSO commands or subcommands.

NOCONLIST — Prevents display of CLIST statements at the terminal.

SYMLIST — Displays all executable statements at the terminal before substitution of any variables. CLIST statements and TSO commands and subcommands are all executable statements.

NOSYMLIST — Prevents display of TSO commands and subcommands and CLIST statements.

MSG — Displays system informational and/or error messages issued by the system from execution of CLIST statements and TSO commands and subcommands.

NOMSG — Prevents display of system messages.

MAIN — Specifies the main command procedure in the user's CLIST environment. It is the highest level when nesting of CLIST procedures is used. MAIN will prevent flushing of the stack if an interrupt or error occurs. If MAIN is specified, FLUSH and NOFLUSH will be ignored. MAIN is not appropriate in nested command procedures.

CAPS — Character strings entered by a user and read by a READ statement or text in a WRITE or WRITENR statement are converted to all upper case.

ASIS — READ character strings or WRITE text is not converted to upper case.

END(string) — Specifies a character string that is to be recognized as an END statement in a DO group. The string must be 1 to 4 alphanumeric characters, and the first character must be alphabetic. The term END is a subcommand to end some TSO commands such as EDIT, while the CLIST statement END means either an end of a DO group or an exit from the CLIST. Any occurrence of END in a DO group terminates the group, not the CLIST or TSO command. Use of an END(string) eliminates this problem. It should be used in all DO groups.

Examples:

1. ```
CONTROL MAIN PROMPT MSG LIST
```

2. ```
CONTROL NOFLUSH
EXEC NESTED
     CONTROL FLUSH     /* Start of Nested CLIST   */
     .....
     EXIT              /* End of Nested CLIST     */
EXIT
```

3. ```
CONTROL MSG NOPROMPT END(ENDX)
.....
IF &A = &B, THEN DO
              .....
              EDIT X.DATA
              CHANGE * 50 /1/2/
              END   /* End EDIT Command */
         ENDX   /* End DO Group   */
.....
END   /* End CLIST   */
```
```

Notes:

1. The default options for CONTROL are FLUSH, NOPROMPT, NOLIST, NOCONLIST, NOSYMLIST and MSG. The MAIN and END(string) options must be coded to be in effect.

2. When a CLIST is executed in TSO, it is loaded into a system queue referred to as a stack. All executable statements, commands and subcommands are read from the stack. When an attention interrupt or an error condition occurs, the system will flush the command procedure from the stack. Processing is terminated and the remainder of the command procedure is purged from the stack. If NOFLUSH is entered on a CONTROL statement, the system will not flush the stack when an interrupt or error occurs. MAIN may be specified on a CONTROL statement in the highest-level CLIST if nested procedures are used or when there is only one level. MAIN inhibits the system from flushing the highest-level CLIST if an interrupt or error occurs in a lower-level procedure. The lower-level command procedures up to the main level are flushed.

3. If NOPROMPT is active in the user's PROFILE for the TSO session, PROMPT in a CONTROL statement will not enable prompting.

4. The PROMPT and/or LIST options may be invoked when a CLIST is initiated by specifying either or both in an explicit EXEC command. This applies whether the CLIST is executed in TSO or as a nested CLIST within higher-level command procedures.

5. When a CONTROL statement with no operands is issued, the name of each option currently in effect will be displayed at the user's terminal. These options are retained and remain in effect unless changed.

6. An environment defined by CONTROL in a primary CLIST is passed to a nested CLIST or a subprocedure. If a CONTROL statement is executed in the nested CLIST or subprocedure, a new environment is defined. The new environment, however, applies only within the nested CLIST or subprocedure. When the nested CLIST or the subprocedure ends, the CONTROL statement defined for the primary CLIST is again in effect.

9.3   DATA . . . . . ENDDATA

Category: Manage the Operating Environment

Function: The DATA . . . ENDDATA statement begins and closes a group of one or more TSO commands and sub-commands. This prevents the CLIST interpreter from treating them as CLIST statements. Thus, it is simulated transfer of processing to a TSO environment at the DATA statement and return to the CLIST environment at the ENDDATA statement. CLIST statements should not be included in DATA . . . ENDDATA groups because they will fail when the system attempts to execute them as TSO commands or subcommands.

Symbolic substitution of all variables in the DATA group is performed before commands are executed.

Format:
```
DATA
. . . . .
. . . . .
ENDDATA
```

Operands: None

Examples:

```
1. IF &A > 10, THEN DO
              DATA
                    EDIT X.DATA
                    BOTTOM
                    INSERT * &B
                    END SAVE
              ENDDATA
         END
```

Notes:

1. In the example above, the EDIT END SAVE statement is not interpreted as a CLIST statement, but as the END subcommand of EDIT. The DATA . . . ENDDATA delimiters ensure that statements between DATA and ENDDATA will not be treated as CLIST statements. If this feature is not coded, the term "END" terminates the DO group, "SAVE" is not interpreted, EDIT does not end, and the dataset X.DATA is not saved.

9.4 DATA PROMPT . . . . . ENDDATA

Category: Manage the Operating Environment

Function: The DATA PROMPT . . . ENDDATA statement en-
closes the one or more answers to prompts for TSO
commands or subcommands. This statement is used
only when the CLIST is executed in a batch job and
there are any TSO commands or subcommands
where the system could issue a prompt for a required
operand. In a batch job, there is no user to respond to
system prompts, and responses must therefore be
entered as a group in DATA PROMPT . . . ENDDATA.
The statement applies to only one TSO command or
subcommand. Thus, DATA PROMPT . . . ENDDATA
must be coded for each TSO command or subcommand that may cause a prompt.

Format:
```
DATA PROMPT
 . . . . .
 . . . . .
ENDDATA
```

Operands: None

Examples:

```
1. ALLOCATE DA(A.DATA) OLD
   ALLOCATE DA(B.DATA) NEW SP(5,1)
   DATA PROMPT
   track       /* Response to prompt for space units */
   ENDDATA
```

```
2. SET &NAME = B
    . . . . .
   COPY
   DATA PROMPT
   a.data      /* Response to prompt for input name  */
   &name..data /* Response to prompt for output name */
   ENDDATA
```

Notes:

1. DATA PROMPT . . . ENDDATA must not be coded in a CLIST executed in an interactive TSO session.
2. A DATA PROMPT . . . ENDDATA statement must immediately follow the TSO command or subcommand that will issue a prompt for a required operand. It applies only to one command or subcommand. Thus, the statement must be coded for each command or subcommand.
3. If no system prompts will be issued for a command or subcommand, the DATA PROMPT . . . ENDDATA statement is not required and must be omitted.
4. The responses may contain any valid character string and may include variables. Symbolic substitution of variables is done before responses are processed.

9.5   TERMIN

Category: Manage the Operating Environment

Function: The TERMIN statement temporarily passes control to a terminal user. TERMIN suspends execution of the procedure and allows the user to perform commands or other operations.

The TERMIN statement defines one or more character strings. The user selects one of them to enter to return control to the CLIST. A comma may be coded before the delimiter strings to enable the user to return control by sending a null (transmit only).

TERMIN statements should always be preceded by one or more WRITE and/or WRITENR statements to display messages that describe all valid delimiter strings and their intended meaning or usage.

When the user is finished, one of the strings from the TERMIN statement is transmitted by the user to return control to the CLIST. Moreover, the user's reply can be examined to determine which delimiter was chosen. The relative positional number of the chosen delimiter is stored in the system variable

&SYSDLM. When the user returns control by a null, the value of &SYSDLM is 0.

The user may enter any values after the delimiter. The input values are stored in the system variable &SYSDVAL. Input data cannot be transmitted if the user enters a null to return control to the CLIST.

Format: TERMIN $\begin{bmatrix} \text{string1} \\ , \end{bmatrix}$ ... $\begin{bmatrix} \text{stringN} \\ \text{stringN} \end{bmatrix}$

Operands: string — Specifies one or more strings that can be entered by a terminal user to return control to the CLIST. One of the character strings must be chosen and entered by the user.

— Enables the terminal user to enter a null line (transmit only) to return control back to the CLIST procedure. Thus, a comma is a special character string designating that the TSO user may enter a null for that positional delimiter. If no comma is specified for a delimiter, control is returned only when the user enters one of the valid delimiter character strings.

Examples:

```
1. WRITE CONTROL IS BEING PASSED TO YOU
   WRITE WHEN YOU ARE FINISHED, ENTER --->
   WRITE      A NULL WITH NO DATE, AMOUNT OR CODE
   WRITE            IF AMOUNT IS 1 THROUGH 10,
   WRITE    OR
   WRITE       "DONE" IF AMOUNT IS 11 THROUGH 100,
   WRITE       "STOP" IF AMOUNT IS 101 THROUGH 1000,
   WRITE       "QUIT" IF AMOUNT IS MORE THAN 1000
   WRITE             FOLLOWED BY A DATE, AMOUNT AND CODE
   TERMIN , DONE STOP QUIT
```

(The terminal user performs TSO functions and enters the second TERMIN delimiter string and values for a date, an amount and a code.)

```
stop 12/25/91 123 abc
```

(The value of &SYSDLM is 2 since the user used STOP, the second delimiter term. The values in &SYSDVAL are the user input data '12/25/91', '123' and 'abc', which can be accessed using the READDVAL statement. The first value is a date that must be treated as a character string to avoid any arithmetic operations (division) when specified in subsequent statements. CLIST processing will branch to LABEL2.)

```
READDVAL &DATE &AMNT &CODE
GOTO LABEL&SYSDLM
```

(If the user had entered null for the delimiter, the value of &SYSDLM would be 0. The user may not also enter any input data. CLIST processing will branch to LABEL0.)

```
IF &SYSDLM = 0, THEN GOTO LABEL0
```

Notes:

1. If the TERMIN statement has no operands, control is returned to the CLIST only when the user transmits a null line (transmit only).
2. When the user transmits a null, no input data can be returned to the CLIST. &SYDLM is 0 and &SYDVAL will have a null value.
3. TERMIN must not be used if the CLIST will be used in a batch job or invoked under ISPF.

9.6   SET

Category: Define and Assign Variables

Function: The SET statement assigns a value to one variable. The variable may have been previously defined by a SET, GLOBAL, PROC or NGLOBAL statement or is being defined and assigned a value by the SET statement. The variable, either defined earlier or currently, is assigned the value determined by resolving the expression. The variable name and expression must be separated by an EQ or = operator.

The expression may contain a null, alphanumeric or numeric value, arithmetic expression, and built-in functions including strings and/or substrings. The variable itself can be included in the expression if it has been previously defined.

Format: SET variable   [EQ]   expression
                               [=]

Operands: variable   — Designates a symbolic variable name to which a value is to be assigned. If the variable has not been defined already, the SET will define it and assign the value of the expression.

            expression — Specifies any real or null value, a string, substring, built-in function or arithmetic expression that, when resolved, is the variable's value.

Examples:

1. SET &A EQ   /* Set &A to Null */
2. SET &A = ((100 / 10) * 2.5)   /* Set &A to 25   */
3. SET &A EQ (&B + (&C - &D))
4. SET &A = &A + 1   /* Increment &A by 1 */
5. SET &A = &A * &B   /* Multiply &A by &B */
6. SET &A EQ &LENGTH(&STR(DECEMBER 25, 1991))
7. SET &A EQ &STR(DEC &SUBSTR(4:5,&SYSDATE)&STR(,)&YR)

Notes:

1. Only a single variable name may be defined and given a value by a SET statement. An expression cannot be entered as the variable. A value is assigned to one variable in each SET statement. The variable cannot be a built-in function or certain system variables.
2. An ampersand prefix on the variable name is optional but it is suggested that ampersands always be used.

9.7 PROC

Category: Define and Assign Variables

Function: The PROC statement defines a set of any number of symbolic variables that can be passed to the CLIST in the parameter list for an EXEC statement issued in TSO or from within a command procedure to call a nested CLIST. PROC statements are optional but, when used, they must be the first statement in the CLIST. Only one PROC statement may be included in each CLIST.

Format: `PROC n [ positional1 ... positionalN ]`
`[ keyword1(value) ... keywordN(value) ]`

Operands: `n` — One- to five-digit number to specify a count of the positional parameters defined on the PROC statement. This number must be zero if no positional parameters are specified.

`positional` — Establishes one or more positional parameters in sequence that require initial values to be specified in an EXEC statement parameter list when the command procedure is initiated. The system prompts the user to enter values for each positional parameter if the user does not enter them. No prompting is done when the number of positional parameters is zero or if the user enters a value for each.

`keyword` — Specifies, in any order, one or more keyword variables. These may have a default value initially assigned and enclosed in parentheses immediately following the keyword name. Default values may be null by not specifying a value in the parentheses, as in (). The user is not required to enter a value for keyword variables, but may enter a value on the EXEC statement to override default null or explicit values. The user must enter the name of the keyword and an override value enclosed in parentheses.

Examples:

1. No positional or keyword variables are specified.

```
PROC 0
```

2. Two positional and no keyword variables are defined. Values for both positional variables must be entered on the EXEC command or the user must specify a value for them when prompted by the system.

```
PROC 2 PARAM1 PARAM2
```

3. No positional variables are defined, and four keyword variables are defined with a default value for each. The value for KEY1 is a null. The value for KEY2 is the number 123, and the value for KEY3 is the string ABC. The default value in KEY4 includes spaces and a special character # and must therefore be enclosed within single quotes.

```
PROC 0 KEY1() KEY2(123) KEY3(ABC) KEY4('SPEC # CHR')
```

4. Two positional and two keyword variables are defined with a null default value for KEY1 while the integer 1234 is the assigned default value for KEY2.

```
PROC 2 PARAM1 PARAM2 KEY1() KEY2(1234)
```

5. One keyword variable is defined. Since the variable has no default value, it serves as a keyword switch.

```
PROC 0 OPTION
```

Notes:

1. A label cannot be used with a PROC statement, and the statement may not be the target of a branch.
2. Symbolic variables on the PROC statement must not be prefixed with an ampersand. Each reference to these variables elsewhere in the CLIST must be prefixed by an ampersand.
3. Positional parameter names are 1 to 252 characters. The first character must be alphabetic and the rest may be alphanumeric. The values entered on the EXEC statement in positional parameters must be character strings with no delimiters or spaces. The value for a positional parameter must not be null. Positional variables may not have default values.
4. Keyword variable names must be 1 to 31 characters in length. The first character must be alphabetic and remaining characters may be alphanumeric. The values for keyword variables may be either null, numeric or character strings. If a character string includes a delimiter (space or comma) or special character (/, #, %, etc.), it must be enclosed within single quote marks within the parentheses, such as ('DEC 25, 91').

   A keyword variable that is defined without a real or null default value has no associated parentheses and serves as an option. Its value is the variable name when the name is included in an EXEC statement; it is null when the name is omitted.
5. Every positional and keyword variable must have an initial value before the procedure can be invoked. A keyword variable may have a default value of null.
6. Values assigned to positional and keyword variables, either by default or specified on an EXEC statement, may be modified at any time in the command procedure by SET, READ and READDVAL statements.
7. The PROC statement initiates a CLIST and must not be confused with the PROC ... END statement to initiate a subprocedure.

9.8 GLOBAL

Category: Define and Assign Variables

Function: The GLOBAL statement establishes symbolic variable names to be global variables that may be passed to or received from any number of nested CLISTs. The GLOBAL statement must be specified in the highest-level command procedure and must be issued before any of the global variables are used. The highest-level CLIST defines the variables. This CLIST and any CLIST within the hierarchy may set and use the values. Every lower-level CLIST that uses any of the variables must also include a GLOBAL statement before its use in the nested CLIST. The maximum number of global variables that can be referenced in a nested CLIST is the number established on the GLOBAL statement in the highest-level CLIST.

GLOBAL variables are positional, both in the first level and in all lower-level CLISTs. Therefore, a variable in the Nth relative position on any level refers to the same variable in the same positional sequence on every GLOBAL statement for all CLISTs. The names at each level may be different, although the same names on all levels is recommended.

Format: GLOBAL name1 [name2 ..... nameN]

Operands: name   — Symbolic variable names defined in a first-level CLIST and used by CLISTs on the first and every lower level.

Examples:

1st level CLIST:	GLOBAL	name1	name2	name3	name4
2nd level CLIST:	GLOBAL	first	second		
3rd level CLIST:	GLOBAL	parm1	value2	dummy3	parm4
4th level CLIST:	GLOBAL	dummy1	dummy2	dummy3	name4

Notes:

1. Global variables are symbolic variables. Therefore, names must be prefixed by an ampersand (&) except in GLOBAL, READ, READDVAL or SET where it is optional.

2. A nested CLIST that uses only some of the variables must include dummy names in its GLOBAL statement to positionally align its name list with the name list on the GLOBAL statement in the highest-level CLIST. When the nested CLIST requires only the first one or more names in the list, the remaining variables need not be defined in the lower-level CLIST.

9.9   NGLOBAL

Category: Define and Assign Variables

Function: An NGLOBAL statement defines symbolic variables to be used in any one or more subprocedures contained in the CLIST. The term NGLOBAL refers to a "named global" variable. The values in NGLOBAL variables may be passed to or received from any subprocedure within the CLIST. Therefore, they are also shared among subprocedures.

   User variables in a parent CLIST are not available to subprocedures unless they are NGLOBALs. In the same way, user variables in subprocedures are not available to their parent CLIST unless defined as NGLOBAL. NGLOBAL variables must be defined before invoking any subprocedure that uses them.

   NGLOBAL variables are recognized by their name and are therefore not positional. They may be entered on an NGLOBAL statement in any order.

Format: NGLOBAL name1 [name2 ..... nameN]

Operands: name   — Name of the variable to be used as a global variable in subprocedures.

Examples:

```
1.  PROC 0
    .....
    NGLOBAL VAR1 VAR2 VAR3
    SET &VAR1 = 25
    SYSCALL SUB1
    .....
```

```
SYSCALL SUB2
. . . . .
SUB1: PROC 0
      SET &VAR2 = &VAR1 + 10
      END
SUB2: PROC 0
      WRITE Value of Variable # 2 is &VAR2      (35)
      END
```

Notes:

1. A CLIST may contain only one NGLOBAL statement. The statement is coded in the primary CLIST and must not be coded in any subprocedures.
2. NGLOBAL variables cannot be used as global variables for nested CLISTs.

9.10   WRITE

Category: Perform Terminal Input/Output

Function: The WRITE statement sends text to be displayed on a user's terminal. This text might consist of any messages, information, prompting requests or other data for the terminal user.

   The WRITE statement causes the terminal's display cursor or type carrier to return to the beginning of a new line after the text is displayed. In the examples below, the character ■ demonstrates the cursor placement after WRITE is executed.

   One or more WRITE (or WRITENR) statements should precede each READ or READDVAL statement. READ and READDVAL statements accept input from the terminal user. Informational messages are usually required to explain to a user the kind of data required for a response and the options available to the user.

Format: WRITE text

Operands: `text`   — Specifies any character string that consists of alphanumeric and numeric characters, system and user symbolic variables and/or expressions.

Examples:

1. ```
   WRITE THE ROUTINE TO COMPUTE AMOUNTS IS BEGINNING
   Display: THE ROUTINE TO COMPUTE AMOUNTS IS BEGINNING
   ■
   ```

2. ```
   WRITE The Current Date is &MONTH. &DAY., &YEAR.
   Display: The Current Date is December 25, 1991
   ■
   ```

3. ```
   WRITE Please Select ONE of the Following:
   WRITE Enter 1 if Amount is Less than 100
   WRITE    or 2 if Amount is 100 or More --->
   Display: Please Select ONE of the Following:
            Enter 1 if Amount is Less than 100
            or 2 if Amount is 100 or More --->
            ■
   READ &ANSWER
   IF &ANSWER IS 1, THEN GOTO SMALL
                    ELSE GOTO LARGE
   ```

Notes:

1. See the discussion and notes on WRITENR statements.

9.11   WRITENR

Category: Perform Terminal Input/Output

Function: The WRITENR statement sends text to be displayed on a user's terminal. The text may consist of any messages, information, prompting requests or other data for the terminal user.

A WRITENR statement causes the terminal's display cursor or type carrier to remain at the end of the
   ```

text rather than move it to the next line. In the examples below, the character ■ demonstrates the cursor placement after WRITENR is executed.

One or more WRITENR (or WRITE) statements should precede each READ or READDVAL statement. READ and READDVAL statements accept input from the terminal user. Informational messages are usually required to explain to a user the kind of data required for a response and the options available to the user.

Format: WRITENR text

Operands: text   — Specifies any character string that consists of alphanumeric and numeric characters, system and user symbolic variables and/or expressions.

Examples:

1. WRITENR Enter YES to Continue or NO to Terminate:
   Display: Enter YES to Continue or NO to Terminate :■

2. WRITE Please Select ONE of the Following:
   WRITE Enter 1 if Amount is Less than 100
   WRITENR   or 2 if Amount is 100 or More --->
   Display: Please Select ONE of the Following:
            Enter 1 if Amount is Less than 100
            or 2 if Amount is 100 or More --- >■

3. WRITENR Please Select ONE of the Following:
   WRITENR Enter 1 if Amount is Less than 100
   WRITENR   or 2 if Amount is 100 or More --->
   Display: Please Select ONE of the Following :■Enter 1
            if Amount is Less than 10 0■   or 2 if Amou
            nt is 100 or More --- >■

Notes:

1. Also refer to the discussion of the WRITE statement, and the READ and READDVAL statements.

2. By default, the system converts all letters in WRITE and WRITENR statements to upper case. Conversion is governed by the CAPS or ASIS operands on the CONTROL statement. Therefore, when the text to be displayed includes lowercase letters, a CONTROL statement and an ASIS operand must be executed before the WRITE or WRITENR statement. The alternative method is to set the system variable &SYSASIS to ON.

3. The system does not perform arithmetic operations on expressions in text in WRITE and WRITENR statements. Therefore, when the message includes any expressions that must be arithmetically resolved before the text is displayed, the expression must be resolved by the system built-in function &EVAL.

   For example, when &A is 5 and &B is 2, the statement

   ```
   WRITE The factored quantity is &A * &B
   ```

   displays the following message.

   ```
   The factored quantity is 5 * 2
   ```

   When the expression is resolved by &EVAL in the text in the WRITE statement

   ```
   WRITE The factored quantity is &EVAL(&A * &B)
   ```

   the following message is displayed.

   ```
   The factored quantity is 10
   ```

4. If consecutive WRITENR statements are executed, each display will follow the last on the same line of the terminal. The messages wrap around to the next line if they are longer than the terminal width. This is normally not a desirable display and is confusing to the user. Most often when multiple messages will be displayed, only the last message is displayed by the WRITENR statement and all preceding messages should be displayed by the WRITE statement.

9.12   READ

Category: Perform Terminal Input/Output

Function: The READ statement accepts one or more values that are entered by a terminal user. The input is used as values for symbolic variables. These variables may have been previously established in the CLIST or are being established with the READ statement.

Specification of variables on a READ statement is optional. If no variables are specified, input is stored in the system variable &SYSDVAL. To access the values entered by a user, a READDVAL statement must be executed.

A WRITE or WRITENR statement normally precedes the READ statement to indicate to the user the kind of input expected and what options are available.

Terminal input may consist of a character string, a numeric value or a null value. When the character string includes special characters or spaces, the complete string must be enclosed in single quotes. A null value is entered by either two consecutive commas (,,) or single quotes (''').

Any mix of one or more types of input may be given for a single READ statement. Each value in a user response must be separated by spaces or commas.

Format: `READ [ variable1 variable2 ... variableN ]`

Operands: `variable`   —   Identifies one or more symbolic user variables. If multiple variables are specified, they are positional since values entered by the terminal user are set into the variables on a READ statement in a sequential order.

Examples:

1. ```
   WRITE Enter the Month, Day and Year
        User: DEC 25 1991
   READ &MONTH &DAY &YEAR
   ```

2. ```
   WRITE Enter the Month, Day and Year
        User: DEC 25 1991
   READ                    /* Input Stored in &SYSDVAL */
   READDVAL &MONTH &DAY &YEAR
   ```

Notes:

1. Also refer to the discussions on READDVAL, WRITE and WRITE statements and the system variable &SYSDVAL.
2. Input received from a terminal user is automatically converted to upper case. This is the default option on the CONTROL statement. When translation to upper case is not wanted, a CONTROL statement with an ASIS operand must be executed before the READ statement.

   Alternatively, the system variable &SYSASIS could be set to ON.
3. When variables are not included on a READ statement, all of the values transmitted by the user are stored in the system variable &SYSDVAL. They are retrieved by the READDVAL statement. Any number of values can be accepted and retrieved in this manner.

9.13 READDVAL

Category: Perform Terminal Input/Output

Function: The READDVAL statement separates the values in the system variable &SYSDVAL into syntactical strings. These values are then assigned in sequential order to the symbolic variables entered on the READDVAL statement. Syntactical strings are defined as any character string, numeric value, value with spaces or special characters (enclosed in single quotes), or null value. A null value is represented by two consecutive commas (,,) or single quotes ('').

The values in &SYSDVAL can originate either from a READ statement with no variables specified or from a TERMIN statement when the user enters data after the TERMIN delimiter. If a subsequent READDVAL is executed, values stored in &SYSDVAL are assigned, in positional order, to the variables named on the READDVAL statement.

When more variables are specified in READDVAL than there are values in &SYSDVAL, the excess variables are assigned a null value. When &SYSDVAL

has more values than are entered on the READDVAL statement, the excess values are ignored.

Format: `READDVAL [ variable1 variable2 ... variableN ]`

Operands: `variable` — Identifies one or more user symbolic variables. If READDVAL has multiple variable names, they are positional. Each value in &SYSDVAL is associated with the variables on READDVAL based on their relative position.

Examples:

1.  ```
    WRITE Enter Item, Rate and Quantity
       User: AB123 1.50 500
    READ                    /* Input Stored in &SYSDVAL */
    READDVAL &ITEM &RATE &QUAN
    WRITE Total for Item &ITEM is &EVAL(&RATE*&QUAN)
    ```

2.  ```
    TERMIN STOP DONE QUIT
       User: DONE AB123 1.50 500
    READDVAL &ITEM &RATE &QUAN
    WRITE Total for Item &ITEM is &EVAL(&RATE*&QUAN)
    ```

Notes:

1. READDVAL is ignored when it has no variable names.

9.14   LISTDSI

Category: List Dataset Information

Function: The LISTDSI statement retrieves information about dataset allocation, characteristics, location and space utilization. LISTDSI must indicate the name of a dataset, or a file name under which the dataset is currently allocated.

Items of information about the dataset consist of allocation specifications, the physical attributes of the dataset such as record length and dataset organization, and volume where the dataset resides as well as its disk space utilization. The items are stored as values in 25 system variables designated for this purpose. Each of these LISTDSI variables is discussed in Chapter 8.

The values in these variables can be used in CLIST expressions and condition tests, and in any number of TSO commands that refer to dataset allocation and characteristics.

Format: LISTDSI

$$\left[\begin{array}{l}\texttt{dataset name} \\ \texttt{filename FILE}\end{array}\right] \quad \left[\begin{array}{l}\texttt{VOLUME(serial)} \\ \texttt{PREALLOC}\end{array}\right]$$

$$\left[\begin{array}{l}\texttt{DIRECTORY} \\ \underline{\texttt{NODIRECTORY}}\end{array}\right] \quad \left[\begin{array}{l}\texttt{RECALL} \\ \texttt{NORECALL}\end{array}\right]$$

Operands:

dataset name — Specifies the name of one dataset on which to retrieve information.

filename — Specifies the file name assigned for a dataset. This is a symbolic name used when the dataset was allocated in an earlier TSO command.

FILE — Keyword to indicate that the name is a file name and not a dataset name. The keyword FILE is mandatory if the name is for a file. When a dataset name is used, FILE must be omitted.

VOLUME(serial) — Specifies a disk volume where the dataset resides and where "serial" is a 1- to 6-character volume identifier. Normal LISTDSI operations search the system's catalogs for a dataset, and VOLUME is used only for uncataloged datasets. When FILE is coded, this operand must not be specified and is ignored if coded.

PREALLOC

— Specifies that a dataset is already allocated, thus avoiding searching in catalogs to determine the dataset's location. PREALLOC may be used only if name is a dataset name. If FILE is coded, PREALLOC will be ignored.

DIRECTORY

— Specifies that LISTDSI determine the number of members and the number of allocated and used directory blocks in a partitioned dataset (library). The dataset must be opened to read its directory, and processing will be slower than if NODIRECTORY is coded.

NODIRECTORY

— Requests that the directory will not be examined and statistics about the members and directory blocks are not retrieved. This is the default.

RECALL

— Recalls (restores) the dataset when it is migrated by HSM (Hierarchical Storage Manager). The dataset will be recalled from any migration level and from any device where a migrated dataset resides.

NORECALL

— Does not recall a migrated dataset. Therefore, statistics about the dataset are not available.

Examples:

1. `LISTDSI ABC.DATA`

2. `LISTDSI LIBR FILE PREALLOC NODIRECTORY RECALL`

Notes:

1. Complete descriptions of 25 LISTDSI system variables are provided in Chapter 8.
2. When neither RECALL nor NORECALL is coded, a migrated dataset will be recalled provided it is stored on a disk volume online on the system.
3. The RECALL and NORECALL options apply only when dataset migration is performed by HSM or an equivalent.
4. If DIRECTORY is specified but the user does not have read authority, NODIRECTORY is in effect.

9.15 OPENFILE

Category: Perform Dataset Input/Output

Function: The OPENFILE statement opens an online file. Once opened, records in an existing file may be read or updated and records may be written to a new file. Thus, an online file can be opened for input, for update or for output based on the mode specified on the OPENFILE statement.

Format:
```
OPENFILE  filename   ┌ INPUT  ┐
                     │ OUTPUT │
                     └ UPDATE ┘
```

Operands: `filename` — Specifies the file name assigned for a dataset. This is a symbolic name used when the dataset was allocated in an earlier TSO command. The file name is used as a variable name when reading, writing and updating a file with GETFILE and PUTFILE statements, and for closing it with the CLOSFILE statement. The file name is not the physical name of the dataset.

INPUT — Specifies that the file is opened to read input records only.

OUTPUT — Specifies that the file is opened to write output records only.

UPDATE — Specifies that the file is opened to read input records, to write output records or to read and write records in the same file. It allows records to be read, modified and rewritten in place in the same file.

Examples:

1. `ALLOCATE FILE(INP) DATA(OLD.DATA) SHR`

   (The ALLOCATE statement is a TSO command to allocate the dataset named OLD.DATA using the file name INP before it is opened by OPENFILE.)

   ```
   OPENFILE INP INPUT      /* Open Input Filename INP */
   GETFILE INP             /* Read One Input Record   */
   SET &VAR = &INP         /* Move Input to Variable  */
   . . . . .
   CLOSFILE INP            /* Close Input File        */
   ```

2. `ATTRIB A DSORG(PS) LRECL(80) BLKSIZE(6240)`
   `ALLOCATE FILE(OUT) DATA(NEW.DATA) NEW USING(A)`

   (ATTRIB and ALLOCATE are TSO commands. ATTRIB defines attributes for an 80-character sequential dataset. ALLOCATE creates a new disk dataset named NEW.DATA using the attributes named "A".)

   ```
   OPENFILE OUT OUTPUT     /* Open Output Filename OUT */
   . . . . .
   SET &OUT = &VALUE       /* Move Value to Variable   */
   PUTFILE OUT             /* Write One Output Record  */
   CLOSFILE OUT            /* Close Output File        */
   ```

3. `ALLOCATE FILE(UPD) DATA(OLD.DATA) SHR`

(The ALLOCATE statement is a TSO command to allocate an existing file that is opened for updating.)

```
OPENFILE UPD UPDATE    /* Open Update Filename UPD */
GETFILE UPD            /* Read One Record as Input */
.....
SET &UPD = &VALUE      /* Move Changes to Variable */
PUTFILE UPD            /* Rewrite Record into File */
CLOSFILE UPD           /* Close Update File        */
```

Notes:

1. Also refer to GETFILE, PUTFILE and CLOSFILE.
2. The default is INPUT when a mode is not specified.
3. The file name must not be prefixed with an ampersand on an OPENFILE statement, but must have an ampersand prefix when used as a variable in other statements.
4. The dataset must be allocated to the user's session before it can be opened. When a new dataset is allocated, its attributes must be defined by either an ATTRIB or ALLOCATE TSO command before it can be opened by OPENFILE.
5. The use of CLIST statements to read, write or update online files is inefficient to perform file input or output. For files with few records, this is not an important consideration. For files of many records, other programming techniques should be used.

9.16 GETFILE

Category: Perform Dataset Input/Output

Function: The GETFILE statement reads one record from a file already opened for INPUT or UPDATE by the OPENFILE statement. GETFILE reads only one record for each execution of the statement. When multiple records are to be read, GETFILE may be executed any number of times by a DO loop. Moreover, records are read only in sequential order beginning with the first. When an Nth record is needed, all records from the first to the Nth are read by GETFILE in a DO loop.

The file name operand of the GETFILE statement is a variable. When GETFILE is executed, the value in the file name variable is the record just read. It can then be used as any other user variable.

Format: `GETFILE filename`

Operands: `filename` — Specifies the file name for the dataset previously opened by an OPENFILE statement. It must be identical to the file name used when the dataset was allocated and opened. It is the symbolic name for the file, not the physical name of the dataset.

Examples:

```
1.  OPENFILE OLD INPUT      /* Open Input Filename OLD */
    DO WHILE &LASTCC = 0    /* Start of DO Group       */
        GETFILE OLD         /* Read One Input Record   */
        SET &RCD = &OLD     /* Put Record in Variable  */
        . . . . .
    END                     /* End of DO Group         */
    CLOSFILE OLD            /* Close Input File        */
```

Notes:

1. Also see the discussion on the OPENFILE, PUTFILE and CLOSFILE statements.
2. The file name must not be prefixed with an ampersand on a GETFILE statement. It must be prefixed with an ampersand if used as a variable in other statements.
3. An end-of-file condition occurs when the last record in the file has been read and another read operation for the file is attempted. A return code of 400 is stored in &LASTCC. Test &LASTCC for 400 after every GETFILE to determine when an end of the file occurs.

9.17 PUTFILE

Category: Perform Dataset Input/Output

Function: The PUTFILE statement writes one record to a file that was previously opened as UPDATE or OUTPUT by an OPENFILE statement. The PUTFILE statement will write only one record each time it is executed. If multiple records are to be written, PUTFILE may be executed any number of times in a DO group.

The file name operand of the PUTFILE statement is a variable. The value in the variable is the record that will be written by PUTFILE. Therefore, this value must be set before PUTFILE is executed. The update or output values must be reset before every PUTFILE execution unless the same record is to be written more than once to the same file.

Format: `PUTFILE filename`

Operands: `filename` — Specifies the file name for the dataset previously opened by an OPENFILE statement. It must be identical to the file name used when the dataset was allocated and opened. It is the symbolic name for the file, not the physical name of the dataset.

Examples:

```
1.  OPENFILE NEW OUTPUT       /* Open Output Filename NEW */
    .....
    SET &NEW = &VALUE         /* Store Value in Variable  */
    PUTFILE NEW               /* Write Output Record      */
    CLOSFILE NEW              /* Close Output File        */

2.  OPENFILE UPD UPDATE       /* Open Update Filename UPD */
    GETFILE UPD               /* Read Record as Input     */
    SET &VALUE = &UPD         /* Store Record in Variable */
    SET &VALUE = .....        /* Modify Record            */
    SET &UPD = &VALUE         /* Store Value in Variable  */
    PUTFILE UPD               /* Update Record in File    */
    CLOSFILE UPD              /* Close Update File        */
```

Notes:

1. Also refer to OPENFILE, GETFILE and CLOSFILE.
2. The file name must not be prefixed with an ampersand on a PUTFILE statement. It must be prefixed with an ampersand if used as a variable in other statements.

9.18   CLOSFILE

Category:	Perform Dataset Input/Output
Function:	The CLOSFILE statement closes an online file that was previously opened by an OPENFILE statement.
Format:	CLOSFILE filename
Operands:	filename — Specifies the file name for the dataset previously opened by an OPENFILE statement. It must be identical to the file name used when the dataset was allocated and opened. It is the symbolic name for the file, not the physical name of the dataset.

Examples:

1.
```
ALLOCATE FILE(ABC) DATA(OLD.DATA) SHR
ATTRIB A DSORG(PS) LRECL(80) BLKSIZE(6160)
ALLOCATE FILE(XYZ) DATA(NEW.DATA) NEW USING(A)
```

(ALLOCATE and ATTRIBUTE are TSO commands to allocate the dataset OLD.DATA, to define attributes for the 80-character sequential file, and to allocate a new dataset NEW.DATA using the attributes named "A".)

```
OPENFILE ABC INPUT     /* Open Input Filename ABC  */
OPENFILE XYZ OUTPUT    /* Open Output Filename XYZ */
GETFILE ABC            /* Read One Input Record    */
SET &XYZ = &ABC        /* Move Input to Output     */
PUTFILE XYZ            /* Write One Output Record  */
CLOSFILE ABC           /* Close Input File         */
CLOSFILE XYZ           /* Close Output File        */
```

Notes:

1. Also refer to OPENFILE, GETFILE and PUTFILE.
2. The file name must not be prefixed with an ampersand on CLOSFILE statements. It must be prefixed with an ampersand if used as a variable in other statements.
3. Datasets must be closed before the CLIST ends. When not closed, it remains open and it could be unusable for subsequent use. Datasets cannot be opened when they are already open. CLOSFILE must be executed on every open file before the CLIST ends. Moreover, a CONTROL statement with the NOFLUSH operand should be in effect to prevent the CLIST from being flushed in case an interrupt or error condition occurs.

9.19   IF–THEN–ELSE

Category: Establish Conditional Action

Function: The IF and THEN statement defines a test condition and determines if that condition is true or false. If the condition is true, the action specified for the THEN operand is executed. If the condition is false, the THEN action is not executed.

Optionally, an ELSE operand may be included in the IF statement. An action specified in ELSE will be executed only if the test condition is false.

An action to be executed for either or for both of the THEN and ELSE operands may consist of only one CLIST statement, one TSO command or subcommand, or one null command.

When more than one operation is to be executed for a THEN or an ELSE action, they must be enclosed in a DO group.

Format: ```
IF comparison THEN action1
            [ELSE action2]
```

Operands:    comparison — A comparative expression consisting of the comparison between two values and/or expressions. A condition
```

may consist of more than one comparative expression connected by the logical operators AND and OR.

THEN — Indicates the start of the action to be taken if the condition is true.

ELSE — Indicates the start of an action for a false condition. The ELSE operand is optional.

action — One CLIST statement, one TSO command or subcommand, one null command, or a DO group of any number of statements and/or commands.

Examples:

```
1.  IF &A EQ &B, THEN GOTO LABEL1
```

```
2.  IF &A EQ &B, THEN                /* Null Command /*
                ELSE GOTO LABEL1
```

```
3.  IF &A EQ &B, THEN +
                IF &A LT &C, THEN DO
                             .....
                             END
                        ELSE DO
                             .....
                             END
           ELSE +
           IF &A GT &C, THEN GOTO LABEL1
```

```
4.  IF (&A>&B) AND (&A<&C) OR ((&X+&Y) = (&Z+10)) +
        THEN DO
             .....
             END
        ELSE GOTO LABEL1
```

Notes:

1. The THEN action and an ELSE action must not be coded on the same line. The following coding is invalid.

```
IF condition THEN GOTO LABEL1 ELSE GOTO LABEL2
```

This IF statement is valid only when the ELSE action is on a separate line, as in this corrected statement.

```
IF condition THEN GOTO LABEL1
              ELSE GOTO LABEL2
```

2. A continuation character is mandatory if the THEN or ELSE operand is continued onto the next line.

```
IF condition +
    THEN +
        GOTO LABEL1
    ELSE +
        GOTO LABEL2
```

3. Multiple conditions may be specified for the IF test, as shown in Example 4 above. Multiple tests must be connected by the logical operators AND and OR.
4. An IF statement may be the action to be executed for either a true or false action. When an IF statement is the THEN or ELSE action, it is nested. There may be any number of levels of nested IF statements. If the number of nested IF statements is more than three or so, the complexity of the coding could easily become unmanageable.

9.20   DO . . . . . END

Category: Establish Conditional Action

Function: The DO and END statements collect CLIST statements and/or TSO commands and subcommands into a group of logically related operations. This forms a DO group. The DO statement denotes the beginning and the END statement denotes the end of the group.
             Each time the DO statement is invoked, each of

the operations within the DO group are executed once. All instructions are performed unless the DO group includes a conditional or unconditional branch out of the loop, or an interrupt or error occurs.

The instructions in a DO group can be executed any number of times by specifying either a WHILE or an UNTIL operand. The DO loop is repeatedly executed as long as a WHILE condition is true or terminates when an UNTIL condition is true. The DO group can also be executed based on the value of a variable. This variable is incremented or decremented by the value defined on the DO statement. Execution will continue until its value exceeds a defined limit.

One or more DO groups may be nested in one or more levels of hierarchy. Thus, a DO group may contain one or more subordinate DO groups. These may also contain subordinate DO groups, and so on.

DO groups are most often the action to be executed as the actions for IF–THEN–ELSE statements and in the routines in ATTN and ERROR statements.

The DO group must be closed with an END statement. However, END also closes CLISTs and subprocedures, and is the subcommand to terminate the TSO command EDIT, OUTPUT and TEST. The term END can be easily misinterpreted. Therefore, redefining the DO loop END statement as a different character string on a CONTROL statement is highly recommended. Examples of alternative END character strings include "ENDX", "ENDR" or any other non-reserved term. The following coding demonstrates defining and using an alternative character string for END.

```
CONTROL END(ENDX)
  . . . . .
  . . . . .
DO  . . . . .
  . . . . .
ENDX
```

Format:
```
DO [ variable = term1 TO term2 BY term3 ]
   [ WHILE condition ]
   [ UNTIL condition ]
. . . . .
END
```

There are four forms of DO group structures. Structure of the DO group determines the number of times that it is executed and specifies the conditions that cause the group to be executed or to be bypassed. The structures are described in detail below.

Single Execution

The format for a DO statement for single execution is the simple DO with no operands. All statements in the DO group are executed only once. Execution is not conditional.

```
DO
```

Iterative Execution

The DO statement format for iterative execution is DO followed by a variable = term1 clause. This is followed by a mandatory "TO" clause. The optional "BY" clause is the last operand on the statement.

```
DO variable = term1 TO term2 BY term3
```

All of the statements in the DO group are executed once or any number of times. Repetitive execution ends only when the value for a variable identified in the DO statement exceeds the limit specified in that DO statement. In other words, execution will continue so long as the value of the variable does not exceed a given integer number.

The initial value of the variable is the evaluated result of the expression entered above as "term1". This expression can be any whole number, or it can be an arithmetic expression including any integers and/or variables whose value is an integer so long as the result of the expression is an integer.

The limit that ends execution of the DO group can be any integer or arithmetic expression that gives an integer when evaluated. This limit is shown as "term2" above. A limit is required and is defined in the "TO" clause of the DO statement.

The control variable's value can be incremented or decremented automatically by any integer or by any expression that, when evaluated, gives an integer. This integer can be any positive or negative whole number. This incrementing expression is specified above as "term3". Automatic control is defined in the "BY" clause of the DO statement. "BY" clauses are optional, and the default increment is +1.

Testing of the control variable is executed before the DO group is executed. When its value does not exceed the limit specified in the "TO" clause, the DO group is executed. If it does, the DO group is not executed. The control variable may exceed the limit the first time the test is conducted. If it does, the DO group is not executed.

Operands:

variable — A predefined user variable whose value is tested each time the DO group is to be executed. The variable is incremented or decremented before the DO is executed.

term1 — Whole number or expression that results in an integer when evaluated. Its value is used to initialize the control variable and it is therefore the first in the range of variable values.

TO term2 — Whole number or expression that results in a positive or negative integer when resolved. It is the limit for the control variable. When the value of the control variable exceeds the limit specified for term2, the group is not executed.

BY term3 — Whole number or expression that results in a positive or negative integer when resolved. The number will increment or decrement the control variable. If "BY" is omitted, the default is to increment by +1.

Conditional Execution

The DO statement format for conditional execution is DO and either a WHILE clause or an UNTIL clause specifying a condition test to determine if the DO group is to be executed.

```
DO [ WHILE condition
     UNTIL condition ]
```

A WHILE clause means that the DO group is executed so long as the specified condition is true. Thus, when the condition is true, the group is executed. However, if the condition is false, execution will be bypassed and processing continues with the next statement after its END statement.

The test condition is tested before each iteration of executing the group. Therefore, it is possible that the DO group would not be executed at all. A condition may be false before the first attempt to execute the DO group.

An UNTIL clause means that the execution of the DO group occurs only if the condition is false. When the test condition is not true, the DO group will be executed. However, when the condition is true, the group is not executed and processing continues with the statement following its END statement.

The test condition is tested after every iteration of executing the group. Therefore, the group will always be executed at least once. This occurs the first time processing flows through the statements in the DO group. After this first iteration, the system performs the test condition. If false, the DO group is executed again. But, when it is true, processing continues with the following statements and does not return to execute the DO group again.

A variable specified in a WHILE or UNTIL condition test is normally modified within the DO group. If the control variable is not incremented or altered in some manner, its value remains constant and the result of the comparison will not change. Thus, a DO group will not terminate. Of course, the group may include conditional and unconditional branches out of the DO group by an embedded GOTO statement.

Operands: WHILE — Specifies that the DO group is to be executed only if the test condition is true.

UNTIL — Specifies that the DO group is to be executed only if the test condition is false.

condition — The comparative condition consisting of a comparison between two expressions or values resulting in either true or false. Conditions can consist of two or more comparisons connected with one or more of the logical operators AND and OR.

Compound Conditional Execution

The DO statement format for compound conditional execution consists of DO followed by a combination of two or more iterative and conditional operands. This combination may consist of both the WHILE and UNTIL conditional tests. Or it can consist of the iterative test with either one or both conditional tests. All syntax, format and operands of each of these tests apply. Finally, if the iterative test is included in the compound conditions, it must be coded before the WHILE or UNTIL operands.

All of the following combinations are valid.

```
DO   WHILE condition
     UNTIL condition

DO   variable = term1 TO term2 BY term3
     WHILE condition

DO   variable = term1 TO term2 BY term3
     UNTIL condition
```

```
DO    variable = term1 TO term2 BY term3
      WHILE condition
      UNTIL condition
```

Examples:

1. *Single Execution—The DO group is executed once only.*

```
DO
      SET &MONTH = &SUBSTR(1:2,&SYSDATE)
      SET &DAY = &SUBSTR(4:5,&SYSDATE)
      SET &YEAR = &SUBSTR(7:8,&SYSDATE)
      WRITE &MONTH &DAY &YEAR
END
```

2. *Conditional Execution—The variable A is assigned a value of 10 before the DO WHILE statement executes. The group is executed since A is greater than 0. In the DO group, the variable A is decreased by –2 each time it is executed. When the DO group is executed five times, A will be decreased to a value of 0, the test condition A > 0 is false, and DO group execution terminates.*

```
SET &A = 10
DO WHILE &A > 0    /* DO Executed 5 Times */
      . . . . .
      . . . . .
      SET &A = &A - 2    /* Decrement &A by 2    */
ENDX
```

3. *Iterative Execution—The variable A is assigned its initial value of 10 by the DO expression &A = 10 and is incremented by 15 in the "BY" clause. The values of B and C (3 and 5) are assigned by SET statements. Since the "BY" expression is &B*&C, the increment is 3 times 5 or 15. The DO is executed until A exceeds the limit in the "TO" clause expression ((&D*2)+50. This limit is 25 times 2 (50) plus 50, that is, 100. In summary, the control variable A is initialized at 10, then incremented by 15 for each iteration of the DO group. The*

value of A before each iteration will therefore equal 10, 25, 40, 55, 70, 85, 100 and 115. Since 100 is not more than 100, the DO group will be executed seven times. Execution ends when the value of A is 115.

```
SET &B = 3
SET &C = 5
SET &D = 25
DO &A = 10 TO ((&D*2)+50) BY (&B*&C)
     IF &RATE > 10 THEN DO
                              . . . . .
                         ENDX
       . . . . .
   ENDX
```

Notes:

1. The iterative execution DO statement is available in TSO/Extensions only. WHILE clauses are available in earlier versions of TSO, but the UNTIL clause may be used only in TSO/Extensions. And last, the compound conditional DO is available only in TSO/Extensions.
2. The string specified in a CONTROL statement for the END(string) operand should be used instead of END.
3. Variables specified in the comparison of a WHILE and an UNTIL conditional execution DO group normally are modified by one or more statements encoded in the DO group. It is necessary to either change the results of evaluating a test condition from true to false or include an unconditional or conditional GOTO branch out of the DO group. Otherwise, the group will have no condition or exit by which to terminate the loop.

9.21   SELECT–WHEN–OTHERWISE–END

Category: Establish Conditional Action

Function: The SELECT–WHEN–OTHERWISE–END statement will test multiple conditions. It executes the actions specified in the first occurrence of a WHEN clause whose condition is true. The actions specified in the WHEN clause may be any single CLIST statement, TSO command or subcommand, a null command, or a DO group of multiple statements and commands.

The SELECT statement is similar to coding multiple IF statements. The IF statement tests a condition and, if true, executes an defined action. If more than one condition is to be tested, each must have an IF statement. The SELECT statement enables the same facility with a single statement using a WHEN clause for each condition. In addition, SELECT is more powerful since it can test a range of values.

The SELECT statement may have any number of two or more WHEN operands. The condition on the WHEN has to be enclosed within parentheses and be separated from the term WHEN by a space.

An optional OTHERWISE operand may be included in a SELECT statement following all WHEN operands. The OTHERWISE operand defines an action to be executed if no WHEN test condition is true. The action for the OTHERWISE clause may be one CLIST statement, a TSO command or subcommand, a null command, or a DO group of multiple statements and commands.

An END statement must terminate the SELECT. Since END can be confused with an END CLIST statement or an END TSO subcommand, a CONTROL statement with an END operand should be used to define the character string for END.

The selection of a WHEN action depends on either of two forms of the SELECT statement. An optional expression may be specified for the SELECT clause.

When the test expression is omitted, the condition test for each WHEN operand evaluates values and/or expressions using one of the comparison operators. The result of the test must be true or false. The action associated with the first condition that is true is executed even though subsequent conditions may also be true.

In the following example, no expression is entered

for the SELECT clause. Each WHEN operand includes a complete test condition. Any of the comparison operators may be used.

```
SELECT
   WHEN (&A = 100) action
   WHEN (&A > &X) action
   WHEN (&A < (&Y + &Z)) action
END
```

When an expression is coded for the SELECT clause, it serves as an implied expression in every one of the WHEN clauses. However, the comparison test is for an equality. Thus, the condition is true only when the SELECT expression equals an expression in the WHEN clause. However, this form of the SELECT statement is more flexible and powerful in that an expression may be compared to multiple expressions connected by the logical operator OR. It can also be compared to a range of low to high values that are coded with a colon (:).

In the following example, an expression is entered for the SELECT operand. In the first WHEN clause, the SELECT variable &A is compared to the variable &X in the WHEN clause and, if equal, the condition is true and the specified action is executed. In the second WHEN, &A is compared to both the integer 10 and the variable &X. If &A is equal to either one as specified by the OR (I) operator, the condition is true and the action is executed. In the third, the variable &A is compared to the variable &X, to the sum of &Y and &Z (&Y+&Z), and to a range from 10 to the value of &B. When &A is equal to any of these values or expressions, the condition is true and the associated action is executed.

```
SELECT &A
   WHEN (&X) action
   WHEN (10 | &X) action
   WHEN (&X OR (&Y+&Z) OR 10:&B) action
END
```

Format:
```
SELECT [ expression ]
            WHEN (condition1) action
            WHEN (conditionN) action
            OTHERWISE         action
END
```

Operands: expression — An optional expression consisting of any value or expression. When used, it is compared to the expressions in each WHEN operand. These conditions may contain any comparison operator.

WHEN — Defines the action to be executed if the associated condition is true.

condition — If the optional expression on SELECT is omitted, tests if a comparison of two values or expressions is true.

If an expression is specified on the SELECT operand, tests if it is equal to the expression in the WHEN clause and, if equal, the test condition is true. The WHEN condition may be any value, expression or a range. Terms in a range must be joined by a colon with the low value first.

OTHERWISE — Defines the action to be executed if no WHEN condition is tested as true. The OTHERWISE operand is optional.

action — Specifies one CLIST statement, a TSO command or subcommand, null command or DO group of multiple commands and statements.

Examples:

1. *Select the action that translates the number of the current month to the name of the month.*

```
SELECT &SUBSTR(&STR(1:2,&SYSDATE))
   WHEN (1) SET &NAME = JANUARY
   WHEN (2) SET &NAME = FEBRUARY
   .....
   WHEN (11) SET &NAME = NOVEMBER
   WHEN (12) SET &NAME = DECEMBER
   OTHERWISE WRITE Month is not 1 through 12
END
```

2. *Select operations to be executed for the end-of-year processing in December, for quarterly processing for March, June or October, or for monthly processing in any other month.*

```
CONTROL ..... END(ENDX)
.....
SET &MONTH EQ &SUBSTR(&STR(1:2,&SYSDATE))
SELECT &MONTH
   WHEN (12) +
        DO
                    WRITE Processing End of Year
                    GOTO ENDYEAR
        ENDX
   WHEN (3 OR 6 OR 9) +
        DO
                    WRITE Processing End of Quarter
                    GOTO QUARTER
        ENDX
   OTHERWISE WRITE Processing End of Month
ENDX
```

Notes:

1. SELECT statements are used in TSO/Extensions only.

9.22 EXEC

Category: Control Execution Sequence

Function: EXEC is a TSO command, not a CLIST statement.

An EXEC command invokes execution of a CLIST. The command may be issued in TSO or may be included in a command procedure to invoke a nested CLIST. The EXEC command can also be issued as a subcommand of EDIT, but the invoked CLIST may contain only EDIT subcommands and CLIST statements.

An EXEC command may have three formats: explicit, implicit and extended implicit. Explicit is used when the command EXEC, EX or EXECUTE is explicitly specified. Explicit execution is mandatory when a dataset name does not have the CLIST qualifier or to invoke LIST/NOLIST or PROMPT/ NOPROMPT options.

The implicit and extended implicit formats may be used only if the dataset that contains the CLIST is a member of a partitioned dataset named with a CLIST qualifier that is currently allocated to the SYSPROC file. In implicit execution, only the PDS member name of the CLIST is required to initiate a CLIST. Extended implicit execution requires only the member name of the CLIST and limits the search for the CLIST only in SYSPROC files to provide the fastest method to initiate a command procedure.

Format:

Explicit Execution

```
EXEC dsname ' [ positional ][ keyword ] '

        ┌  PROMPT   ┐ ┌  LIST   ┐
        │ NOPROMPT  │ │ NOLIST  │
        └           ┘ └         ┘
```

Implicit Execution

```
membername [ positional ][ keyword ]
```

Extended Implicit Execution

```
%membername [ positional ][ keyword ]
```

Operands: dsname — Designates the name of a sequential dataset or member of a partitioned dataset that contains the CLIST to be invoked by explicit execution. If the dataset's descriptive qualifier is not CLIST, the name must be fully qualified and enclosed in a pair of single quote marks. Examples of the use of fully qualified names are:

```
'userid.MYPROC.CLIST'
'userid.MYPROC.CLIST(MEMBER)'
'userid.MYPROC.DATA'
```

Examples of unqualified names are:

```
MYPROC.CLIST
MYPROC.CLIST(MEMBER)
```

Examples of dataset names where the qualifier CLIST is implied are:

```
MYPROC
MYPROC(MEMBER)
```

An example of a partitioned dataset whose name is 'userid.CLIST' is:

```
(MEMBER)
```

membername — Designates the name of a member of a partitioned dataset containing the procedure to be invoked by implicit execution. The member must be in a dataset named 'userid.CLIST' that is currently allocated to SYSPROC. The TSO command consists solely of a membername and parameters; "EXEC" is implied and must be omitted.

%membername — Designates the name of a member of a partitioned dataset containing the procedure to be invoked by extended implicit execution. The member must be in a 'userid.CLIST' dataset that is currently allocated to SYSPROC. The TSO command consists solely of a membername (prefixed with a percent sign) and any parameters. "EXEC" is implied and must be omitted.

positional — Enters a list of one or more values specified by the CLIST user that are substituted for symbolic variables in the PROC statement in the CLIST. A value must be entered for each of the positional variables and must be in the same sequential order as in the PROC statement. The system will not start the CLIST until a value is given for every positional variable. Values must be specified either when the CLIST is executed or in response to prompts by the system.

keyword — Enters a list of one or more values specified by the user that override default values specified for keyword variables in the PROC statement in the CLIST. Values for keywords need not be entered by the user. If they are, the name of the keyword must be given, and the new value is enclosed in parentheses. Keyword values may be entered in any order. The system does not prompt the user to enter a value for variables not specified as the CLIST is initiated, but accepts the PROC statement default values.

PROMPT — Enables the CLIST to prompt the user for input. See notes for CONTROL.

NOPROMPT — Prevents the command procedure from prompting the user even when the TSO session has prompting capabilities.

LIST — Displays TSO commands or subcommands at a terminal after substitution for variables but before execution. It does not display CLIST statements.

NOLIST — Prevents the display of TSO commands and subcommands at the terminal.

Examples:

(In all of the following examples, values entered on an EXEC command are associated with variables on the PROC statement. Some of the examples illustrate the system prompts where the user does not specify values for the positional parameters.)

1. *Explicit execution with no parameters or operands.*

```
EXEC 'userid.MYPROC.CLIST(DATE)'
PROC 0
```

2. *Explicit execution with no positional and no keyword values. The system parameters PROMPT and NOLIST are requested.*

```
EXEC MYPROC.CLIST PROMPT NOLIST
    System: ENTER VALUE FOR MONTH
     User: December
    System: ENTER VALUE FOR DAY
     User: 25
    System: ENTER VALUE FOR YEAR
     User: 1991
PROC 3 MONTH DAY YEAR
```

3. *Explicit execution with a missing positional value.*

```
EXEC (DATE) 'December 1991'
    System: ENTER VALUE FOR YEAR
     User: 1991
PROC 3 MONTH DAY YEAR
```

(This execution is in error in that the user omitted a value for DAY in the EXEC command. The value for DAY is 1991. The system prompts for the "missing" YEAR, and the CLIST user enters 1991. The resulting date will be an erroneous December 1991 1991.)

4. *Implicit execution with two override keyword values.*

```
DATE DAY(25) MONTH(Dec)
PROC 0 MONTH(December) DAY() YEAR(1991)
```

5. *Extended implicit execution without the one required positional value and one override keyword value.*

```
%DATE YEAR(1991)
    System: ENTER VALUE FOR WEEKDAY
     User: MONDAY
PROC 1 WEEKDAY MONTH(DECEMBER) DAY(25) YEAR()
```

Notes:

1. All values for positional and/or keyword values when an explicit EXEC command is issued must be enclosed within a single pair of quote marks. If implicit or extended implicit execution is specified, parameters are not enclosed in quote marks.
2. A PROMPT option in effect for higher-level CLISTs is not automatically in effect for nested CLISTs. This operand is, however, the default. Also, if NOPROMPT is in effect on a main CLIST but prompting is needed in the nested CLIST, it may have a CONTROL statement with the PROMPT option. PROMPT or NOPROMPT could be entered on an explicit EXEC statement for the nested CLIST.
3. The EXEC command is also entered as EX or EXECUTE.

9.23 END

Category: Control Execution Sequence

Function: The END statement ends a command procedure. When the system encounters the END statement, execution of the CLIST is terminated.

When END is executed in a nested CLIST, control is passed to the next higher level command procedure. Control returns to TSO when the END statement in a main or the highest level CLIST is executed.

Format: END

Operands: None

Examples:

```
1. PROC 0                   /* Start Main CLIST    */
   . . . . .
   EXEC NEST1               /* Start NEST1 CLIST   */
   . . . . .
   END                      /* Terminate NEST1 CLIST */
   . . . . .
   END                      /* Terminate Main CLIST  */
```

2. `TESTER: IF &A EQ &B, THEN GOTO FINISH`

   `.....`

   `.....`

   `FINISH: END`

Notes:

1. In order to ensure consistency and to avoid possible confusion with an END statement in a DO group or the END subcommand of EDIT, OUTPUT or other TSO command, it is suggested that EXIT statements be used instead of END to terminate a command procedure.
2. An END statement may be executed anywhere within the command procedure. END may therefore be a statement within a DO group, the action operand of conditional statements, a labeled statement to which a branch is made, and within any other executable routine.
3. Multiple END statements may be included in the CLIST to terminate the procedure in different routines.
4. Also refer to discussions of the END(string) operand on the CONTROL statement and its use in DO–END and SELECT statements.

9.24   EXIT

Category: Control Execution Sequence

Function: The EXIT statement ends a main or nested CLIST and control returns to the next higher CLIST or TSO.

   A return code can be issued when the CLIST ends if a CODE operand is specified. The return code must be an integer from 0 to 4095 or an expression that yields a value from 0 to 4095 when resolved. When a CODE operand is omitted, the return code will be the value in the system variable &LASTCC.

   The QUIT option specifies that control will bypass every higher-level nested CLIST until one with the CONTROL option MAIN or NOFLUSH occurs or, if there are no parent CLISTs with these options, to TSO.

Format: EXIT [CODE(expression)] [QUIT]

Operands: CODE(expression) — Specifies a value or expression whose value is 0 to 4095. The value is issued as a return code.

QUIT — Bypasses higher-level CLISTs in the hierarchy to a CLIST with NOFLUSH or MAIN in effect or to TSO if none.

Examples:

1. PROC 0   /* Start of Main   */
    CONTROL MAIN
    EXEC NEST1

        PROC 0   /* Start of NEST1 */
        CONTROL NOFLUSH
        EXEC NEST2

            PROC 0   /* Start of NEST2 */
            CONTROL FLUSH
            EXEC NEST3

                PROC 0   /* Start of NEST3 */
                CONTROL FLUSH
                EXIT QUIT   /* Exit from NEST3 */

            EXIT   /* Exit from NEST2 */

        EXIT   /* Exit from NEST1 */

    EXIT CODE(&A+4)   /* Exit from Main */

In the preceding example, the optional QUIT operand on the NEST3 EXIT statement bypasses the NEST2 CLIST and processing returns directly to NEST1. Since the EXIT statement in NEST1 does not specify the operand QUIT, processing passes to the MAIN CLIST when NEST1 terminates. When MAIN termi-

nates, processing passes to TSO. The EXIT statement in the MAIN CLIST issues a return code by the CODE operand. The value of the code is the result of the expression &A + 4.

Notes:

1. In order to ensure consistency and to avoid possible conflict with the END statement in a DO group or the END subcommand of EDIT, OUTPUT or other commands, it is recommended that an EXIT statement be used rather than END to terminate a command procedure.
2. An EXIT statement may be executed anywhere within a command procedure. EXIT could therefore be included within a DO group, the action operand of conditional statements, a labeled statement to which a branch is made, and within any other executable routine.
3. Multiple EXIT statements may be contained in a CLIST to terminate the procedure in different routines.
4. Also refer to discussions of the END(string) operand on the CONTROL statement and its use in DO–END and SELECT statements.

9.25 GOTO

Category: Control Execution Sequence

Function: The GOTO statement causes a branch within a CLIST. When a GOTO statement is executed, control passes to an executable CLIST statement or TSO command or subcommand with a label. This label is the target of the GOTO. The target for the branch must be an executable statement, not a comment or blank line. The statement is executed, and processing continues from the new location.

The GOTO statement may be an unconditional branch. Alternatively, it may be conditional as the action in an IF or SELECT statement test condition.

Format: `GOTO label`

Operands: label   — Specifies either a literal label or an expression that can be reduced to a valid label when resolved.

Examples:

1. `IF &A > &B, THEN GOTO LABEL1`

2.
```
XX: SET &X EQ &SUBSTR(1:2,&SYSTIME)
    IF &X < 12, THEN GOTO AM
                ELSE GOTO PM
AM: WRITE GOOD MORNING
    GOTO PROCESS
PM: WRITE GOOD AFTERNOON
    GOTO PROCESS
```

3.
```
XX: IF &SUBSTR(1:2,&SYSTIME) < 12, THEN SET &LAB = A
                                   ELSE SET &LAB = P
    GOTO &LAB.M
AM: WRITE GOOD MORNING
    GOTO PROCESS
PM: WRITE GOOD AFTERNOON
    GOTO PROCESS
```

Notes:

1. GOTO may not branch into or out of a nested CLIST or a subprocedure, nor between subprocedures. GOTO must not branch to a subprocedure PROC statement.
2. The label must be the first operand on the statement to which the branch is directed and must be followed by a colon (:). The target statement must contain a CLIST statement or a TSO command.

9.26   PROC . . . . . END

Category: Perform CLIST Subprocedures

Function: The PROC . . . END statement identifies and labels a CLIST subprocedure. Similar to the PROC statement for a main CLIST, the subprocedure PROC statements define all parameters that could be passed to them by SYSCALL statements. Either or both positional and keyword parameters may be specified, just as on the CLIST PROC statement.

The syntax and function of PROC . . . END statements is identical to the PROC statement that initiates a main or nested CLIST. However, do not confuse a subprocedure PROC statement with a CLIST PROC.

The first statement in every subprocedure must be a PROC statement. It must be assigned a label for identification. This label is a mandatory operand on a SYSCALL statement to invoke the subprocedure.

Each subprocedure must close with an END statement to indicate the end of the routine.

Format:
```
label: PROC n [ positionall ... positionalN ]
               [ keywd1(value) ... keywdN(value)  ]

       . . . . .
       END
```

Operands:

n — One- to five-digit number designating a count of the positional parameters defined on the PROC statement. This number must be zero if no positional parameters are specified.

positional — Establishes one or more positional parameters in sequence that require initial values to be included on the SYSCALL statement parameter list for invoking the subprocedure. Since no prompting is done, a value for every positional parameter is required.

keywd(value) — Specifies, in any order, one or more keyword variables. These may have a default value initially assigned and enclosed in parentheses immediately following the keyword name. Default values may be null by not specifying a value in the parentheses, as in (). Override values are specified on the SYSCALL statement.

Examples:

```
1.  MAIN: SET &VAR EQ &STR(XYZ)
          SYSCALL SUB1 123 456 KEY2(&VAR)
          . . . . .
          EXIT
    SUB1: PROC 2 POS1 POS2 KEY1(ABC) KEY2(DEF)
          . . . . .
          END
```

Notes:

1. Subprocedures and the PROC . . . . END statement can be used only under TSO/Extensions.

9.27   SYSCALL

Category: Perform CLIST Subprocedures

Function: The SYSCALL statement invokes and executes a CLIST subprocedure. A subprocedure can be invoked from any point within the main CLIST and may be invoked any number of times. The subprocedure consists of all statements beginning with PROC and terminating with END.

The name of the subprocedure is the label assigned to the subprocedure's PROC statement. This is the name by which SYSCALL statements must identify the subprocedure to be executed.

A subprocedure may also include SYSCALL statements to invoke nested subprocedures.

SYSCALL statements may also specify positional

and keyword values for a subprocedure's PROC statement. When PROC statements define positional parameters, every SYSCALL statement to invoke the subprocedure must supply a value for each positional parameter. Keyword parameters may also be defined on the PROC statement with a real or null default value. This default value is overridden by entering a value on the SYSCALL statement to invoke the subprocedure.

The process of passing values to variables defined on the PROC statement is logically the same as the capability to specify values on an EXEC command to be passed to positional and keyword variables on a PROC statement for a CLIST.

The variables on a SYSCALL statement are unique to that statement's execution. That is, they are not automatically available to any nested subprocedure invoked from within subprocedures. Variables that are to be shared by two or more subprocedures must be defined as NGLOBAL variables.

Format: `SYSCALL subprocname [positional] [keyword(value)]`

Operands: `subprocname` — Specifies the name of a subprocedure to be invoked. It must be the label on the PROC statement of the invoked subprocedure.

            `positional` — Specifies the values to be passed to the one or more positional variables on a subprocedure's PROC statement. A value must be entered for each of the positional variables and must be in the same sequential order as in the PROC statement. An error occurs if a value is not provided for every positional parameter.

keyword(value) — Specifies override values to be passed to one or more keyword variables on the PROC statement for the subprocedure. The name of the variable is required, and an override value is enclosed in parentheses. The keyword values may be coded in any order on the SYSCALL statement.

Examples:

```
1. MAIN: SET &A = 25
         SYSCALL SUB1 &A 123 KEY1(ABC) KEY2(&A+10)
         . . . . .
         SET &B = 10
         SET &C = 50
         SYSCALL SUB1 100 &B+&C
         . . . . .
         EXIT
   SUB1: PROC 2 POS1 POS2 KEY1(XYZ) KEY2(DEF)
         . . . . .
         END
```

Notes:

1. Subprocedures and SYSCALL statements may be executed in TSO/Extensions only.

9.28   SYSREF

Category: Perform CLIST Subprocedures

Function: The SYSREF statement specifies that a string coded on a SYSCALL statement is to be used as a name and not as a variable. Thus, it is not used to pass a value. Values are passed to a subprocedure by the SYSCALL statement. However, this does not provide for passing a value back to the main CLIST when it has been modified in the subprocedure. The SYSREF statement is used to serve this purpose.

A variable whose value is to be passed back to the main CLIST must be specified on a SYSREF statement included within the subprocedure. Only one SYSREF may be contained in a subprocedure but it can name one or any number of variables.

On the SYSCALL statement, the name of the variable is coded but it is not prefixed with an ampersand. Omission of the ampersand prefix specifies that it is the name of the variable and not a variable for passing values. Without the ampersand prefix, the system does not try to resolve it as a variable.

The value of the named variable (named on SYSCALL) is passed by the SYSCALL statement to the executed subprocedure. If the name of the variable is also coded on a SYSREF statement in that subprocedure, its value will be returned to the main CLIST when the subprocedure ends. In this manner, values may be modified in subprocedures. The modified values are made available to the main command procedure.

Format: `SYSREF variable1 ..... variableN`

Operands: `variable` — Specifies the name of a variable on the PROC statement of a subprocedure that corresponds to a variable name on a SYSCALL statement to invoke it.

Examples:

```
  1.  MAIN:  SET &A = 25
             SET &B = 5
             WRITE A plus B is &EVAL((&A+&B)        25 + 5 = 30
             SYSCALL SUB1 &A B
             WRITE A plus B is &EVAL((&A+&B)        25 + 65 = 90
             . . . . .
             EXIT
      SUB1:  PROC 2 VAR1 VAR2
             SYSREF &VAR2
             SET &A = 10
             SET &B = 65
             WRITE A plus B is &EVAL((&A+&B)        10 + 65 = 75
             END
```

Notes:

1. Subprocedures and SYSREF statements are available in TSO/ Extensions only.

9.29 RETURN CODE

Category: Perform CLIST Subprocedures

Function: The RETURN CODE statement will issue a return code back to the main CLIST or other subprocedure that invoked the current subprocedure. The return code must be a whole number or expression that yields a number. This return code is stored in the system variable &LASTCC. When the subprocedure ends, the main CLIST can examine the return code in &LASTCC.

If the term CODE is entered without an expression, &LASTCC is set to a null value.

Processing continues with the next statement after the SYSCALL statement when the subprocedure ends. &LASTCC with the return code value is available to that next statement. However, since the statement also issues its own return code, the subprocedure return code is overridden unless it is immediately saved. This is accomplished by a SET statement to assign the value in &LASTCC to a user variable.

Format: `RETURN CODE(expression)`

Operands: `CODE(expression)` — Specifies a whole number or an expression that resolves to a number to be issued as a return code to the main CLIST or to a subprocedure that invoked the current subprocedure.

Examples:

```
1.  MAIN: SET &VAR = &STR(XYZ)
          SYSCALL SUB1 123 456 KEY2(&VAR)
          SET &SUBRC EQ &LASTCC
          IF &SUBRC > 8, THEN GOTO ERRCODE
          . . . . .
    SUB1: PROC 2 POS1 POS2 KEY1(ABC) KEY2(XYZ)
          . . . . .
          SET &A EQ &X+2
          RETURN CODE(&A+(&B*&C))
          END
```

Notes:

1. Subprocedures and the RETURN CODE statement are used only in TSO/Extensions.

2. The RETURN CODE statement is used only for returning codes from subprocedures. It should not be confused with a RETURN statement for ATTN and ERROR routines.

9.30 ATTN

Category: Manage Errors and Interrupts

Function: Normally, when a terminal user issues an attention interrupt during CLIST execution, CLIST processing is terminated by the system in the same way that a TSO command or subcommand is terminated.

An ATTN statement establishes an environment where an attention interrupt by the terminal user can be intercepted. The ATTN statement defines an action to be executed if the user issues an interrupt.

The action defined for an ATTN routine may consist of any executable CLIST statement or a TSO command or subcommand. Most often, the action consists of a DO group to execute statements and/or commands. The action may be a null command and the attention interrupt is thereby ignored. An ATTN routine may be used to control termination of the procedure.

The ATTN routine may execute only one TSO command. It may be a null command so that no action occurs.

Normally, an ATTN routine is included at the start of the procedure, although it may be entered at any point in the CLIST.

The CLIST interrupt intercept feature is activated and actions for the ATTN routine are defined when processing executes the ATTN statement. Execution of the statements and commands in the ATTN routine occurs, however, only if the user issues an actual attention interrupt subsequent to execution of the ATTN statement to define an interrupt routine.

When OFF is specified, an active interrupt routine is nullified and no routine is defined. If a user issues an interrupt, processing may be terminated depending on the CONTROL MAIN status.

Format: ATTN $\begin{bmatrix} \text{action} \\ \underline{\text{OFF}} \end{bmatrix}$

Operands: action — An executable statement, or a DO group that may include any number of CLIST statements and not more than one TSO command or subcommand.

OFF — Nullifies a prior ATTN statement; a subsequent interrupt could disrupt normal processing.

Examples:

```
1. ATTN DO            /* Attention Routine is in Effect */
   WRITE YOUR ATTENTION INTERRUPT HAS BEEN DETECTED
   WRITE DO YOU WISH TO END ALL PROCESSING (Y OR N)?
   READ &ANSWER
   IF &ANSWER = Y, THEN EXIT
   WRITE PROCESSING IS CONTINUING
   SET &TSOCMD =         /* Set Null TSO Command */
   &TSOCMD               /* Execute Null Command */
   RETURN
   END
```

(When the ATTN statement is executed, the operations in the DO group are active as an attention routine. If the user issues an attention interrupt after the ATTN statement is executed, the attention interrupt routine is executed. Note that the routine has a RETURN statement and that one TSO command must be executed before the RETURN. &TSOCMD is a null TSO command.)

2. `ATTN OFF    /* Interrupt Intercepted and Ignored */`

(When an ATTN OFF statement is executed, any current attention interrupt routine is voided. If the user issues an interrupt, processing will be disrupted.)

Notes:

1. The default is OFF if an action or OFF is not coded.
2. DO groups in an ATTN routine must close with the END statement or with an END string defined in a CONTROL statement.
3. Control is returned to the next statement following the statement where the interrupt was issued if a DO group includes a RETURN statement that is executed.
4. Only one TSO command can be executed in the DO group or as the executable statement in an ATTN routine.
5. One TSO command must be executed before a RETURN can be executed. This requirement applies regardless of the number of executable CLIST statements before the RETURN statement. The required TSO command may be a null command as illustrated by the use of &TSOCMD in Example 1 above.
6. Also see the discussion on the RETURN statement.

9.31   ERROR

Category: Manage Errors and Interrupts

Function: An error condition is any occurrence of a non-zero return code by a CLIST statement, or a TSO command or subcommand. Normally, if an error condition is detected by the system, processing of the CLIST is immediately terminated depending on the severity of the error.

The ERROR statement establishes the environment in which an error condition is intercepted. An ERROR statement defines an action to be executed when an error condition occurs.

An action defined for an ERROR routine may consist of any executable CLIST statement or TSO command or subcommand. Most often, the action consists of a DO group to execute statements and/or TSO commands and subcommands. The action may be a null command so that the system attempts to continue processing at the statement after the one that resulted in an error condition. ERROR routines are also used for controlling termination of the procedure.

Usually, the ERROR routine is coded near the start of the procedure, although it may be entered at any point in the CLIST. The actions to be executed by an ERROR routine are defined when processing flows through the ERROR statement, but are not executed. Execution of the routine occurs only if the system detects an error condition.

The CLIST error intercept feature is activated and actions for the ERROR routine are defined when the ERROR statement is executed. Execution of actions in the routine, however, occurs only if the system detects an error, that is, a non-zero return code.

When the OFF operand is specified, the prior error routine is nullified. Therefore, no special error routines are in effect and the CLIST may terminate if an error condition is detected.

If no executable statements are entered and if the OFF operand is not specified, the system will list both the statement in which the error occurred and applicable explanatory error messages. The system will attempt to continue processing beginning with the next statement.

Format: ERROR $\begin{bmatrix} \text{action} \\ \text{OFF} \end{bmatrix}$

Operands: action   — An executable statement, or a DO group that may include any number of

CLIST statements and/or any number of TSO commands and subcommands.

OFF — Nullifies a previous ERROR statement, and a subsequent error condition may terminate CLIST processing.

Examples:

1.
```
ERROR DO             /* Error Routine is in Effect */
WRITE AN ERROR CONDITION WAS DETECTED IN THE LAST
WRITE OPERATION. DO YOU WISH TO CONTINUE (Y OR N)?
READ &ANSWER
IF &ANSWER = N, THEN EXIT
RETURN
END
```

2.
```
ERROR OFF       /* Nullify Previous Error Routine */
```

3.
```
ERROR           /* List Error and Resume Processing */
```

Notes:

1. There is no default. When neither actions nor OFF is specified, the error statement and appropriate error messages will be displayed and execution of the next statement is attempted.
2. DO groups in an ERROR routine must close with an END statement or with an END string defined in a CONTROL statement.
3. Control is returned to the next statement following the statement where the error occurred if a DO group includes a RETURN statement that is executed.
4. The MAIN or NOFLUSH operand of the CONTROL statement may be in effect in order to prevent the system from flushing the procedure when an error occurs.
5. Also refer to the discussion on the RETURN statement and the CONTROL statement MAIN and FLUSH operands.

9.32   RETURN

Category: Manage Errors and Interrupts

Function: The RETURN statement is included within an ATTN or ERROR routine. Processing is returned to the next statement following the one where an interrupt was issued or where the system detected an error.

Format: RETURN

Operands: None

Examples:

```
1.  ATTN DO
        WRITE YOUR INTERRUPT HAS BEEN INTERCEPTED
        IF ..... THEN DO
                    SET &TSOCMD =      /* Set Null Command */
                    &TSOCMD            /* Execute Null TSO */
                    RETURN
                    END
        END
    ERROR DO
        SET &CODE = &LASTCC
        IF &CODE < 8, THEN RETURN
                        ELSE EXIT
        END
```

(If a user enters an interrupt or if a non-zero code was received from a statement or command, an active ATTN or ERROR routine is processed. If a RETURN is executed by the routine, the system will attempt to resume processing at the next statement.)

Notes:

1. RETURN may be used only in ATTN and ERROR routines.
2. Statements after a RETURN in ATTN and ERROR routines are not executed when RETURN is executed. However, the routine may include a conditional test to branch around the RETURN so that it is not executed.
3. In an ATTN routine, one TSO command must be executed before RETURN is executed. It may be a null command as shown by &TSOCMD in the ATTN statement examples.
4. Also refer to the ATTN and ERROR statements.
5. The RETURN statement is used for only ATTN and ERROR routines. It must not be confused with the RETURN CODE statement for CLIST subprocedures.

9.33 WHEN SYSRC

Category: Manage Errors and Interrupts

Function: WHEN is a TSO command, not a CLIST statement.

The WHEN command tests the return code issued by a program invoked by the CALL or LOADGO command that immediately precedes the WHEN command. SYSRC is a variable whose value is the program's return code. This value is compared to an integer. If the test condition is true, a specified command is executed or processing is terminated. If the condition is false, no action is taken and processing continues with the next statement in the command procedure.

Successive WHEN commands can be used for execution of multiple tests provided they immediately follow the CALL or LOADGO for the subject program.

Format:
```
WHEN SYSRC(operator integer)  ⎡  END    ⎤
                              ⎣ command ⎦
```

Operands:
SYSRC — Contains the return code issued by a program and is compared to a value.

operator — Any of the comparison operators EQ, NE, GT, LT, GE, NG, LE or NL. Their symbolic equivalents may be coded.

integer — Specifies a numeric integer to which the return code is compared.

END — Terminates processing if the test is true. END is the default.

command — Specifies any valid TSO command with appropriate operands to be executed when the test condition is true. If no command is specified, processing terminates since END is the default.

Examples:

```
1.  CALL PROGRAM
    WHEN SYSRC(=0) EXEC NEST1
    WHEN SYSRC(>0) EXEC NEST2


2.  LOADGO MYPGM
    WHEN SYSRC(NE 0) END     /* End If RC is Not = 0 */


3.  LOADGO MYPGM
    WHEN SYSRC(NE 0)         /* End If RC is Not = 0 */
```

Notes:

1. The operand SYSRC must be specified. The comparison operator and integer must be enclosed in parentheses and immediately follow the SYSRC operand.
2. Only TSO commands and/or subcommands may be entered as commands in the SYSRC operand. CLIST statements may not be specified.
3. The WHEN statement may be executed only if the CLIST is in the TSO command/subcommand environment because WHEN is applicable only to test return codes from an execution of programs by either CALL or LOADGO, which are TSO commands. It is also imperative to ensure that a nested CLIST is operating in TSO mode if it includes WHEN statements.
4. The IF–THEN–ELSE statement can perform any tests that a WHEN statement can perform. IF–THEN–ELSE operates in either a TSO or CLIST environment, and it can specify TSO commands and subcommands as well as CLIST statements as its operands.
5. The WHEN TSO command is not related to a WHEN clause on the SELECT statement. WHEN operands for a SELECT statement must be followed by an END statement, which closes the SELECT operation. When the END statement is inadvertently omitted, the WHEN clause for SELECT statements could be misinterpreted.

9.34 EXERCISES

1. Write the one or more CLIST statements needed for each of the requirements below.

    a. Code an EXEC command to execute a CLIST named DOIT. A PROC statement that defines one positional parameter named P1 and two keyword parameters named K1 and K2 is required. The keyword variable K1 has a default value of "XYZ" and K2 has a null default value. The CLIST user will specify "10" as a value for P1, will override the default value for K1 with the new value "ABC", and will issue a value of "DEF" for K2.

    b. Code a CONTROL statement that will list all executable statements as they are executed, that will display all system messages, that can prevent the CLIST from being flushed if an error condition occurs, and that defines an alternative character string for END.

    c. Code a WRITE statement that displays only the current month and day.

    d. Code a SET statement that will set the variable &YEAR to the current year in the system date.

    e. Code an IF statement using the system variable &SYSDSN to determine if a dataset named "userid.ABC.DATA" is available (value "OK"). If it is, execute the LISTDSI statement to determine the dataset characteristics.

f. Code the required SET and GOTO statements to branch to
LAB5. The GOTO statement refers to a label name "LAB"
with the suffix "&N".

_____

_____

g. Code an IF–THEN–ELSE statement that tests if a value is
numeric. If it is, multiply it by 10, and if it is not, branch to
a statement labeled "ERROR". The variable to be tested is
named "&TEST".

_____

_____

_____

h. Execute a compound conditional DO group that examines
each position in a character string named &CHAR either
until a currency sign ($) is found or until the entire string
is examined and no currency sign is found. The search will
start with the LAST position and continues backwards to
the first position. The variable name of the string is
&CHAR and the variable to control the DO loop is named
&CNTR.

_____

_____

i. Code a SELECT statement to branch to LABEL1 if the sum
of &A and &B is less than 10, to LABEL2 if it is less than 50,
or to LABEL3 if it is 50 or more.

_____

_____

_____

_____

2. Create a variable named &ALPH and assign as its value all 26 letters of the alphabet. Then perform a DO group that writes the alphabet to the terminal on two separate lines of 13 letters each.

   Only one WRITE statement may be used in the procedure and it is included in the DO group. Use variable names &CTR1 for the number of times the DO group is executed (twice), and &CTR2 and &CTR3 for substring selection.

   Hint: *Set &CTR2 to 1 and &CTR3 to 13 for the first loop of the DO group, and then increment both counters for the second execution of the DO group.*

   _____

   _____

   _____

   _____

   _____

   _____

   _____

   _____

   _____

3. As three separate operations, request the first name, the middle initial and the last name from the terminal user. Add a period after his or her middle initial when the user has omitted it. Then, create a single character string that consists of the first name, middle initial and last name, including proper spacing.

   Use variable names of &FN for the first name, &MI for the middle initial and &LN for the last name. Use a variable name of &FULL for the user's full name.

---

4. An online dataset is not numbered. In a DO WHILE group, read each record, insert a line number to prefix the data, and write the altered record to a new dataset. However, each input record is to be displayed on the terminal to enable the user to respond with "Y" when the record is to be kept. Therefore, the user can elect to retain or drop records for the output. When the user decides to keep an input record, it is first prefixed with a line number and then written to the output dataset. If the user decides to drop the record, it is simply ignored and the DO group returns to read the next input record.

The first output record is numbered 100 and the number of each successive record is incremented by 100. After all input records are processed, the count of output records is displayed for the user.

Assume that the input and output datasets were allocated previously using the file names OLDFILE for the input and NEWFILE for the output. However, remember that you must first open the files and close them when done.

The variable names are &CNTR to count the output records, &NUMB for the incremental value to number each record, and &LAST to save the return code from each GETFILE. Be sure to test for end-of-file when &LASTCC will be 400, and branch out of the DO group after the last record is read.

_____

_____

_____

_____

_____

_____

_____

_____

_____

_____

_____

_____

_____

_____

_____

_____

_____

_____

_____

_____

_____

CLIST Examples

The three CLIST procedures provided below illustrate the use of many of the features of command procedures. They present excellent examples of proper statement syntax, correct usage of system and user variables, nesting capabilities, terminal input/output, and arithmetic and comparison operations.

These examples do not, of course, demonstrate all statements and operations of the CLIST language. However, examples for all of the features of the language are presented throughout this book. The reader is encouraged to review them as well as these sample procedures.

The sample procedures in this section will execute in an IBM MVS environment. While the "Greeting" and the "Date Names" CLISTs will successfully execute in any current TSO version, the "Text Numbers" CLIST will execute only in TSO/Extensions because it includes subprocedures and an NGLOBAL statement.

Because no external files are employed, no disk datasets or devices are required for successful execution of these three procedures.

The "Greeting" CLIST is the least complicated of these three sample procedures. Its logic is relatively straightforward even though it defines and uses many user variables.

The "Text Numbers" CLIST is of moderate complexity. It uses subprocedures to translate numbers into words. While it has few variables, the procedure is lengthy due to the necessity of examining every position in a number and taking an action based on the value of the number. This, of course, leads to many possibilities, which must all be accounted for.

The "Date Names" CLIST is highly complex. It performs table searches and numerous DO groups, and requires 24 user variables.

10.1   GREETING CLIST

The "Greeting CLIST" displays a greeting to a terminal user. The greeting consists of three message lines. For example:

```
Good Afternoon, Mary
Today is Thursday, July 4, 1991
The time is 3:45:28 PM
```

Text in the first message line is "Good Morning" until 11:59 and "Good Afternoon" at 12:00 noon or later. The message is followed by a comma and the user's name. The Greeting CLIST requests the user to enter his or her name when the procedure is initiated. Users' names might be available in system tables or files used to maintain TSO user identification data. The name could be retrieved from this system information and the user would not need to be prompted. It would also be simple to just eliminate the user's name in the text and avoid this problem by deleting the applicable statements in the CLIST.

The second message line is "Today is . . . " with the complete current date after converting the numeric month and day from the system date to the names of the day and the month. The date is also used for determining the relative number of the day of the week. Monday is referred to as day 1, Tuesday as day 2 and so on until Sunday, which is day 7. This number is then used to determine the name of the current day. And the value of the month in the system date is used in determining the name of the month.

Last, the Greeting CLIST displays a third message line, which states "The time is . . . " where time is based on a 12-hour clock using AM and PM. The procedure translates the time in the 24-hour system clock to the 12-hour standard time.

The following is an outline of the operations performed.

1. Receive user's name from TSO EXEC command
2. Get current date and time from system clock
3. Develop first message line
   — Determine if morning or afternoon
   — Format message
   — Add comma and user's name
4. Develop second message line
   — Determine relative number of day of the week
   — Convert relative number of day to name of day
   — Convert number of month to name of month
   — Format message including names of day and month
   — Add comma after name of day and calendar date
   — Prefix year with "19"
5. Develop third message line
   — Convert 24-hour system clock to 12-hour time
   — Append time with "AM" or "PM"
6. Print three message lines
7. Terminate CLIST procedure

The CLIST defines 17 user variables. These are:

&MSG1	Text for first line
&MSG2	Text for second line
&MSG3	Text for third line
&NAME	Name of the user
&HOUR	Current hour of the day
&CDAY	Current calendar day
&MNTH	Current month
&YEAR	Current year
&AMPM	A if morning or P if afternoon
&FRST	Day of week for first day in month
&CNTR	Reverse counter from current day
&NUMB	Number of day in week for current day
&DAYN	Name of the day
&MONN	Name of the month
&TBL1	This variable contains the relative number of the day of the week for the first day of each month for the year 1990. In 1990, January 1 occurred on Monday (day 1),

February 1 was on Thursday (day 4), and so on until December 1, which was on Saturday (day 7).

&TBL2   This variable contains the names of the days. There are 9 positions for each name including required spaces to allow for the longest name, which is Wednesday.

&TBL3   This variable defines the names of the months with a length of 9 characters for each. This includes spaces to allow for the longest name, which is September.

Note: *The Greeting procedure will not work correctly after February 28, 2004 unless it is modified.*

```
0010 PROC 1 NAME
0020 CONTROL ASIS END(ENDX)
0030 START: SET &HOUR = &SUBSTR(1:2,&SYSTIME)
0040        SET &MNTH = &SUBSTR(1:2,&SYSDATE)
0050        SET &CDAY = &SUBSTR(4:5,&SYSDATE)
0060        SET &YEAR = &SUBSTR(7:8,&SYSDATE)
0070   /*                                                          */
0080   /*  Define tables for day number and names                 */
0090   /*                                                          */
0100 TABLE: SET &TBL1 = 144725736146
0110        SET &TBL2 = &STR(Monday     +
0120                         Tuesday   WednesdayThursday +
0130                         Friday    Saturday Sunday    )
0140        SET &TBL3 = &STR(January   February March    +
0150                         April     May      June     +
0160                         July      August   September+
0170                         October   November December )
0180 DAYNO: SET &FRST = &SUBSTR(&MNTH,&TBL1)
0190        IF &YEAR < 04, THEN +
0200                  SET &YEAR = &YEAR + 100
0210        SET &FRST = &FRST + (&YEAR - 90)
0220        IF (&YEAR = 92 AND &MNTH > 2) OR +
0230           &YEAR > 92 THEN SET &FRST = &FRST + 1
0240        IF (&YEAR = 96 AND &MNTH > 2) OR +
0250           &YEAR > 96 THEN SET &FRST = &FRST + 1
0260        IF &FRST > 7, THEN SET &FRST = &FRST - 7
```

```
0270          SET &CNTR = &CDAY + &FRST
0280          DO WHILE &CNTR > 7
0290               SET &CNTR = &CNTR - 7
0300            ENDX
0310          SET &NUMB = &CNTR - 1
0320          IF &NUMB = 0, THEN SET &NUMB = 7
0330    /*                                                   */
0340    /*  Create message line 1 with greeting             */
0350    /*                                                   */
0360 MESG1: IF &HOUR < 12, THEN SET &AMPM = A
0370                           ELSE SET &AMPM = P
0380          GOTO SET&AMPM.M
0390 SETAM: SET &MSG1 = &STR(Good Morning)
0400          GOTO GREET
0410 SETPM: SET &MSG1 = &STR(Good Afternoon)
0420 GREET: SET &MSG1 = &MSG1&STR(, )&NAME
0430    /*                                                   */
0440    /*  Create message line 2 with date                 */
0450    /*                                                   */
0460 MESG2: SET &MSG2 = &STR(Today is )
0470          SET &DAYN = +
0480             &SUBSTR((&NUMB*9)-8:&NUMB*9,&TBL2)
0490          SET &MSG2 = &MSG2&DAYN&STR(, )
0500          SET &MONN = +
0510             &SUBSTR((&MNTH*9)-8:&MNTH*9,&TBL3)
0520          SET &MSG2 = &MSG2&MONN&STR( )&CDAY
0530          SET &YEAR = &YEAR + 1900
0540          SET &MSG2 = &MSG2&STR(, )&YEAR
0550    /*                                                   */
0560    /*  Create message line 3 with time                 */
0570    /*                                                   */
0580 MESG3: IF &HOUR > 12, THEN +
0590                           SET &HOUR = &HOUR - 12
0600          SET &MSG3 = &STR(The time is )
0610          SET &MSG3 = &MSG3&HOUR
0620          SET &MSG3 = &MSG3&SUBSTR(3:8,&SYSTIME)
0630          SET &MSG3 = &MSG3&STR( )&AMPM.M
0640    /*                                                   */
0650    /*  Print display for terminal user                 */
```

```
0660    /*                                                    */
0670 PRINT: WRITE MSG1
0680        WRITE MSG2
0690        WRITE MSG3
0700        EXIT
```

10.2   TEXT NUMBERS CLIST

The "Text Numbers" CLIST requests the terminal user to enter any number from 0 through 9999. When the user responds with a valid number, the procedure interprets each of its digits. The individual digits are converted into words. The textual form of the user's number is displayed at his or her terminal.

As examples, when the user requests the number 17, the CLIST displays the text "Seventeen". When the user requests 2187, the display is "Two Thousand, One Hundred and Eighty-Seven".

The CLIST examines every position in the user's number. For each position, the corresponding word for the number in that position is determined. This corresponding word is appended to a variable named &TEXT. During the process of assembling the textual character string to be displayed, the CLIST will make appropriate decisions to include or omit a comma and to include the terms "and", "Thousand", and "Hundred". In this manner, the complete text is built by appending terms and by including descriptive qualifiers where needed.

The CLIST employs three subprocedures to convert integers to words. ALPHA converts single integers to the terms "One" to "Nine". SECND translates the values 20, 30, 40, 50, 60, 70, 80 and 90 to the correct terms. Finally, TEENS converts the values 10 through 19 to proper text.

The possible formats of any number from 0 to 9999, where "N" is a digit from 1 to 9 and "0" is zero, are shown here with representative numeric and text examples.

NNNN	1234	One Thousand, Two Hundred and Thirty-Four
NNN0	1230	One Thousand, Two Hundred and Thirty
NN0N	1204	One Thousand, Two Hundred and Four
NN00	1200	One Thousand, Two Hundred
N0NN	1015	One Thousand and Fifteen

N00N	1005	One Thousand and Five
N000	1000	One Thousand
NNN	567	Five Hundred and Sixty-Seven
NN0	560	Five Hundred and Sixty
N0N	507	Five Hundred and Seven
N00	500	Five Hundred
NN	89	Eighty-Nine
N0	80	Eighty
N	9	Nine
0	0	Zero

The following list is an outline of the CLIST operations.

1. Request user to enter a number from 0 to 9999
2. Verify that the user entered a valid reply, that is, the response is a number, and that it is not greater than 9999, not negative and not a null value
3. If response is not valid, issue a message and return to request user to enter a number
4. When the user's number is 0, set text to "Zero"
5. Use three subprocedures to translate digits to text
   — ALPHA converts digits 1 to 9 to "One" to "Nine"
   — SECND converts multiples of 10 (that is, 20, 30, 40 through 90) to "Twenty" to "Ninety"
   — TEENS converts 10 to 19 to "Ten" to "Nineteen"
6. When number is 4 digits, convert thousands digit
   — Set text for digit in thousands position
   — Append text "Thousand"
   — If digit in hundreds position is not zero, add a comma to text
   — If digit in hundreds position is zero and digit in tens or units position is not zero, append an " and " string to text
7. When number is 3 or 4 digits, convert hundreds digit
   — Set text for digit in hundreds position
   — Append text "Hundred"
   — If digit in tens or units position is not zero, append " and " to text
8. When number is 2, 3 or 4 digits, convert tens digit
   — If digit in tens position is 1, set variable for text to "Ten" to "Nineteen" depending upon digit in units position

— If digit in tens position is 2 to 9, set text to "Twenty" to "Ninety" and append "-" if the units position is not zero

9. If number is not zero and digit in units position is 1 to 9, set text to "One" to "Nine"

10. Display text for terminal user and terminate CLIST

The CLIST uses five variables. They are:

&NUMB   Number from 0 to 9999 entered by user
&DIGT   Integer in each position of the number
&TENS   Integers in tens and units position
&WORD   Integer value expressed as a word
&TEXT   Complete textual form of the number

```
0010 PROC 0
0020 CONTROL ASIS END(ENDX)
0030 NGLOBAL &DIGT &WORD
0040    /*                                                      */
0050    /* Request user to enter a number 0 to 9999             */
0060    /* and verify that it is a valid number                 */
0070    /*                                                      */
0080 INPUT: WRITENR Enter a number from 0 to 9999
0090        READ &NUMB
0100        SET &NUMB = &STR(&NUMB)
0110        IF &DATATYPE(&NUMB) = CHAR, +
0120           THEN GOTO NONUM
0130        IF &LENGTH(&NUMB) = 0, THEN GOTO NOENT
0140        IF &NUMB > 9999, THEN GOTO TOOHI
0150        IF &NUMB < 0, THEN GOTO MINUS
0160        GOTO OKNUM
0170 NONUM: WRITE You entered a non-numeric value
0180        GOTO INPUT
0190 NOENT: WRITE You entered only a null value
0200        GOTO INPUT
0210 TOOHI: WRITE You entered a number over 9999
0220        GOTO INPUT
0230 MINUS: WRITE You entered a negative number
0240        GOTO INPUT
0250    /*                                                      */
0260    /* Begin conversion of number to text                   */
```

```
0270   /*                                                          */
0280 OKNUM: WRITE Converting &NUMB to text
0290        WRITE
0300        SET &TEXT =
0310        IF &NUMB = 0, THEN +
0320           DO
0330              SET &TEXT = &STR(Zero)
0340              GOTO PRINT
0350           ENDX
0360        GOTO THOUS
0370   /*                                                          */
0380   /* Convert thousands position if number                    */
0390   /* is 4 digits                                             */
0400   /*                                                          */
0410 THOUS: IF &LENGTH(&NUMB) = 4, THEN +
0420           DO
0430              SET &DIGT = &SUBSTR(1,&NUMB)
0440              SYSCALL ALPHA
0450              SET &TEXT = +
0460                 &STR(&TEXT&WORD&STR( Thousand))
0470              IF &SUBSTR(2,&NUMB) > 0, THEN +
0480                 SET &TEXT = &STR(&TEXT&STR(, ))
0490              ELSE +
0500                 IF &SUBSTR(3:4,&NUMB) > 0, +
0510                    THEN SET &TEXT = +
0520                         &STR(&TEXT&STR( and ))
0530           ENDX
0540   /*                                                          */
0550   /*  Convert hundreds position if number                    */
Q560   /*  is 3-4 digits and position is not 0                    */
0570   /*                                                          */
0580 HUNDR: IF (&LENGTH(&NUMB) = 4 AND +
0590            &SUBSTR(2,&NUMB) > 0) OR +
0600            (&LENGTH(&NUMB) = 3), THEN +
0610           DO
0620              IF &LENGTH(&NUMB) = 4 +
0630                 THEN SET &DIGT = +
0640                         &SUBSTR(2,&NUMB)
0650                 ELSE SET &DIGT = +
```

```
0660                              &SUBSTR(1,&NUMB)
0670                 SYSCALL ALPHA
0680                 SET &TEXT = +
0690                    &STR(&TEXT&WORD&STR( Hundred))
0700                 IF &LENGTH(&NUMB) = 4, +
0710                    THEN SET &TENS = +
0720                             &SUBSTR(3:4,&NUMB)
0730                    ELSE SET &TENS = +
0740                             &SUBSTR(2:3,&NUMB)
0750                 IF &TENS > 0, +
0760                    THEN SET &TEXT = +
0770                             &STR(&TEXT&STR( and ))
0780              ENDX
0790    /*                                                */
0800    /* Convert tens position if number is             */
0810    /* 2-4 digits and position is not 0               */
0820    /*                                                */
0830 TENS:  IF &LENGTH(&NUMB) = 1, THEN GOTO UNITS
0840        SET &DIGT = +
0850            &SUBSTR((&LENGTH(&NUMB)-1),&NUMB)
0860        IF &DIGT = 1, THEN +
0870           DO
0880              SYSCALL TEENS
0890              SET &TEXT = +
0900                 &STR(&TEXT&WORD)
0910              GOTO PRINT
0920           ENDX
0930        IF &DIGT > 1, THEN +
0940           DO
0950              SYSCALL SECND
0960              SET &TEXT = +
0970                 &STR(&TEXT&WORD)
0980              IF &SUBSTR(&LENGTH(&NUMB),&NUMB) +
0990                              > 0, +
1000                 THEN SET &TEXT = +
1010                         &STR(&TEXT&STR(-))
1020                 ELSE SET &TEXT = +
1030                         &STR(&TEXT&STR( ))
1040           ENDX
```

```
1050   /*                                                */
1060   /* Convert units position of number               */
1070   /* if position is not 0                            */
1080   /*                                                */
1090 UNITS: SET &DIGT = +
1100        &SUBSTR(&LENGTH(&NUMB),&NUMB)
1110        IF &DIGT > 0, THEN SYSCALL ALPHA
1120 PRINT: WRITE &TEXT
1130        WRITE
1140        EXIT
1150 ALPHA: PROC 0
1160        SELECT &DIGT
1170            WHEN (1) SET &WORD = One
1180            WHEN (2) SET &WORD = Two
1190            WHEN (3) SET &WORD = Three
1200            WHEN (4) SET &WORD = Four
1210            WHEN (5) SET &WORD = Five
1220            WHEN (6) SET &WORD = Six
1230            WHEN (7) SET &WORD = Seven
1240            WHEN (8) SET &WORD = Eight
1250            WHEN (9) SET &WORD = Nine
1260        ENDX
1270 SECND: PROC 0
1280        SELECT &DIGT
1290            WHEN (2) SET &WORD = Twenty
1300            WHEN (3) SET &WORD = Thirty
1310            WHEN (4) SET &WORD = Forty
1320            WHEN (5) SET &WORD = Fifty
1330            WHEN (6) SET &WORD = Sixty
1340            WHEN (7) SET &WORD = Seventy
1350            WHEN (8) SET &WORD = Eighty
1360            WHEN (9) SET &WORD = Ninety
1370        ENDX
1380 TEENS: PROC 0
1390        SET &DIGT = +
1400            &SUBSTR(&LENGTH(&NUMB),&NUMB)
1410        SELECT &DIGT
1420            WHEN (0) SET &WORD = Ten
1430            WHEN (1) SET &WORD = Eleven
```

```
1440              WHEN (2) SET &WORD = Twelve
1450              WHEN (3) SET &WORD = Thirteen
1460              WHEN (4) SET &WORD = Fourteen
1470              WHEN (5) SET &WORD = Fifteen
1480              WHEN (6) SET &WORD = Sixteen
1490              WHEN (7) SET &WORD = Seventeen
1500              WHEN (8) SET &WORD = Eighteen
1510              WHEN (9) SET &WORD = Nineteen
1520        ENDX
```

10.3 DATE NAMES CLIST

The "Date Names" CLIST generates a simple message consisting of the year, month, day, Julian day, name of the month, name of the day of the week, and the relative day of the week. In addition, the message includes the calculated number of days from Wednesday, January 1, 1975 to the date requested by the user. This computation date is used to easily determine the number of days between any two dates even when they are many years apart. Finally, "Date Names" determines when the year in the specified date is a leap year.

Sunday is considered to be the first day of the week. Thus, Monday is day 2, Tuesday is day 3, and so on until Saturday, which is day 7.

The term Julian date, as used in these procedures, does not refer to the Julian calendar, but rather to the form for the date as "yyjjj" where yy is the year and jjj is the relative number of days in the year beginning with January 1. March 15, for example, is Julian day 74 for common years and 75 in leap years. A Julian day, when used in computer processing, is normally treated as a three-digit number with leading 0's for dates before day 100.

The basis of all this information is a date specified by the user. This date specification is entered as a response to a query issued by the procedure. The date may be specified as any Gregorian (mm/dd/yy) or Julian (yyjjj) date from January 1, 1975 to December 31, 1999. The user also has the option to enter no date (null value) and the procedure will use the current system date as the date specification.

Although the CLISTs have been thoroughly documented, a brief discussion of their general operation follows.

The procedure consists of a main CLIST named "DATEPRNT" that requests a date from the user, invokes a subordinate, nested CLIST named "DATECALC", and displays the messages. The CLIST "DATECALC" performs all of the calculations and translations to convert dates and to determine names of months and days.

"DATEPRNT" is the main, highest-level CLIST procedure and is invoked in TSO simply by explicit or implicit execution. It defines all of the global variables used in both CLISTs. It first displays the current system date for information only. The CLIST then requests the terminal user to enter either a Gregorian (mm/dd/yy) or Julian (yyjjj) date or to enter null (transmit only) if the current date is to be used. The user response is read and tested to determine if the user entered a null value to request data for the current system date.

"DATEPRNT" then displays the specified or current date. The nested CLIST named "DATECALC" is then invoked to compute all of the required data. The date is passed to "DATECALC" as a positional parameter. All computed data is then returned to "DATEPRNT" as global variables. "DATEPRNT" issues a message to display a simple heading plus a second message to display all of the computed data items.

"DATECALC" is an invoked CLIST procedure. Its purpose is to calculate all of the required information. First, it sets a series of variables consisting of the first and last days in every month for both common and leap years. Next, it sets a table with 0 indicating common years and 1 specifying a leap year. Then, it sets variables with the names for the months and the weekdays.

"DATECALC" then tests the date received from "DATEPRNT". If the value in the first two positions is greater than 12, the requested date must be a Julian date. When the value is not more than 12, the date must be a Gregorian date.

If a Julian date has been specified, the items for Gregorian dates (year, month, day, leap year) are generated. When the request is for a Gregorian date, the items for a Julian date (year, Julian day, leap year) are calculated.

For either Julian or Gregorian dates, the next routines will determine the computation date, the relative day of the week and the names of the month and day. When every item for the report is generated, "DATECALC" ends and processing returns to "DATEPRNT" to print the report.

All lines of coding in the CLIST examples below are properly numbered. The many comments not only document the functions of the routines and statements that immediately follow, they serve to segment the CLISTs into easily readable sections.

The CLIST uses 24 variables. They are:

&DATEX   The date requested by the user or the system date if the user did not specify a date

Nine global variables are defined in the CLISTs. Their values are determined in "DATECALC" and returned to the main "DATEPRNT" procedure, which displays them.

&YEAR	2-digit year
&MONTH	2-digit month
&DAY	2-digit day
&JDAY	3-digit Julian day
&MONTHN	Name of month (JAN through DEC)
&DAYN	Name of day (SUN through SAT)
&RELDAY	Relative number of day in week (1 through 7)
&LEAPYR	YES for leap years and NO for common years
&CMPDAY	Number of days since January 1, 1975

Seven variables are defined and used as tables in CLIST "DATECALC". These variables are examined as substrings to select, for example, the applicable name of a month.

&TBL1	Relative day from January 1 for last day for each month in common years (031 to 365)
&TBL2	Relative day from January 1 for last day for each month in leap years (031 to 366)
&TBL3	Relative day from January 1 for last day for preceding month in common years (000 to 334)
&TBL4	Relative day from January 1 for last day for preceding month in leap years (000 to 335)
&TBL5	Leap years (1) or common years (0) 1975–1999
&TBL6	3-character name of the month
&TBL7	3-character name of the day of the week

There are seven miscellaneous variables. They are used to control DO loop execution, to store interim results, and to extract values such as the appropriate name of a month from user variables used as tables.

&CALDAY   Interim number of days computed as requested day plus number of days in every prior month to calculate Julian day when user requests a Gregorian date

&CNTR   Used to select starting and ending positions in TBL1 or TBL2 to examine Julian days

&LOOP   Used to count the number of times a DO group is executed to set variables to: (1) select a substring in TBL1 or TBL2 for Julian days, or (2) select the number of calendar days in the month when computing the Julian day

&LPYR   0 if common year or 1 if leap year specified in TBL5 for common and leap years

&MONTBL   Number of calendar days in each month

&SWCH   Used as a switch in DO group to continue the search for Julian day in TBL1 or TBL2 and to terminate DO group when Julian day is found

&TEST   Value of Julian days in TBL1, TBL2, TBL3 and TBL4 to determine the number of the previous month and the requested month (1 to 12)

The following presents what the user sees at his or her terminal. In the illustration below, the character ■ presents cursor placement after the WRITENR statement is executed to request a response from the user.

This example shows a user request for a Gregorian date.

```
DATEPRNT
12/25/91
ENTER DATE AS MM/DD/YY OR YYJJJ
     OR HIT TRANSMIT FOR TODAY :  ■ 12/25/88

FOR 12/25/88

YEAR MONTH DAY JDAY MONTHN DAYN RELDAY LEAPYR CMPDAY
 88    12   25  360  DEC    SUN    1     YES    5108

READY
```

This example shows a user request for a Julian date.

```
DATEPRNT
12/25/91
ENTER DATE AS MM/DD/YY OR YYJJJ
      OR HIT TRANSMIT FOR TODAY : ■ 90359

FOR 12/25/90

YEAR MONTH DAY JDAY MONTHN DAYN RELDAY LEAPYR CMPDAY
 90    12   25  359   DEC   TUE    3     NO    5838
READY
```

This example shows a null response to use the current date.

```
DATEPRNT
12/25/91
ENTER DATE AS MM/DD/YY OR YYJJJ
      OR HIT TRANSMIT FOR TODAY : ■

FOR 12/25/91

YEAR MONTH DAY JDAY MONTHN DAYN RELDAY LEAPYR CMPDAY
 91    12   25  359   DEC   WED    2     NO    6197
READY
```

DATEPRNT Main Command Procedure

```
0010 PROC 0
0020 CONTROL END(ENDX)
0030 GLOBAL +
0040    YEAR MONTH DAY JDAY MONTHN DAYN RELDAY LEAPYR CMPDAY
0050       /* Display current system date             */
0060       WRITE &SYSDATE
0070    /*********************************************/
0080    /* READ ---                                  */
0090    /*     Request date specification from user  */
0100    /*                                           */
```

```
0110 READ: WRITE ENTER DATE AS MM/DD/YY OR YYJJJ
0120       WRITENR       OR HIT TRANSMIT FOR TODAY :
0130       READ &DATEX
0140       /* Set user date to character string          */
0150       SET &DATEX = &STR(&DATEX)
0160       /* Test if answer is null                      */
0170       /* Use system date if so                       */
0180       IF &LENGTH(&DATEX) = 0, +
0190           THEN SET &DATEX = &STR(&SYSDATE)
0200       /* Set user or system date to character string */
0210       SET &DATEX = &STR(&DATEX)
0220       /* Write blank line, user date, blank line     */
0230       WRITE
0240       WRITE FOR &STR(&DATEX)
0250       WRITE
0260       /****************************************************/
0270       /* NEST ---                                     */
0280       /*     Invoke nested CLIST "DATECALC"           */
0290       /*     with user input date as parameter        */
0300       /*     to compute date information              */
0310       /*,                                             */
0320 NEST: EXEC (DATECALC) '&DATEX'
0330       /****************************************************/
0340       /* PRNT ---                                     */
0350       /*     Display heading and date information      */
0360       /*                                              */
0370 PRNT: WRITE YEAR MONTH DAY JDAY MONTHN +
0380             DAYN RELDAY LEAPYR CMPDAY
0390       WRITE &YEAR    &MONTH   &DAY  &JDAY    &MONTHN +
0400             &DAYN    &RELDAY       &LEAPYR   &CMPDAY
0410       /****************************************************/
0420       /* FINI ---                                     */
0430       /*     Write blank line and quit                */
0440       /*                                              */
0450 FINI: WRITE
0460       EXIT
```

DATECALC Nested Command Procedure

```
0010 PROC 1 DATEX
0020 CONTROL END(ENDX)
0030 GLOBAL +
0040    YEAR MONTH DAY JDAY MONTHN DAYN RELDAY LEAPYR CMPDAY
0050 SET &DATEX = &STR(&DATEX)
0060    /***************************************************/
0070    /* TABL ---                                        */
0080    /*      Set tables for --                          */
0090    /*          TBL1 TBL2    last day of current month, */
0100    /*          TBL3 TBL4    last day of prior month,  */
0110    /*          TBL5        leap years (1975-1999),    */
0120    /*          TBL6        names of months            */
0130    /*          TBL7        names of days              */
0140    /*                                                 */
0150 TABL: SET &TBL1 = +
0160           &STR(031059090120151181212243273304334365)
0170       SET &TBL2 = +
0180           &STR(031060091121152182213244274305335366)
0190    /* Last day in prior month                         */
0200       SET &TBL3 = +
0210           &STR(000031059090120151181212243273304334)
0220       SET &TBL4 = +
0230           &STR(000031060091121152182213244274305335)
0240    /* Leap years from 1975 to 1999 are 1              */
0250       SET &TBL5 = &STR(01000100010001000100001000)
0260       SET &TBL6 = JANFEBMARAPRMAYJUNJULAUGSEPOCTNOVDEC
0270       SET &TBL7 = SUNMONTUEWEDTHUFRISAT
0280    /***************************************************/
0290    /* CHEK ---                                        */
0300    /*      Test 1st 2 characters of date              */
0310    /*      If 1 - 12, user reply is a Gregorian date  */
0320    /*      If > 12, user reply is a Julian date       */
0330    /*                                                 */
0340 CHEK: IF &SUBSTR(1:2,&DATEX) > 12, THEN GOTO JULN
0350       GOTO GREG
0360    /***************************************************/
```

```
0370    /* JULN ---                                              */
0380    /*      Convert input Julian date to Gregorian           */
0390    /*                                                        */
0400    /*      Set Month, Day, Year,                             */
0410    /*          Julian Day and Leap Year                     */
0420    /*                                                        */
0430 JULN: SET &YEAR = &SUBSTR(1:2,&DATEX)
0440      SET &JDAY = &SUBSTR(3:5,&DATEX)
0450      SET &LPYR = &SUBSTR(&YEAR-74,&TBL5)
0460      SET &SWCH = 0
0470      SET &LOOP = 0
0480      SET &CNTR = 0
0490      /* Perform loop until Julian day is found       */
0500      /*      in TBL1 or TBL2                          */
0510      /* Relative position (value of LOOP) is         */
0520      /*      the number of the month 1 - 12           */
0530      DO WHILE &SWCH < 1
0540        SET &CNTR = ((&LOOP * 3) + 1)
0550        IF &LPYR = 0, +
0560          THEN SET &TEST = +
0570                        &SUBSTR(&CNTR:&CNTR+2,&TBL1)
0580          ELSE SET &TEST = +
0590                        &SUBSTR(&CNTR:&CNTR+2,&TBL2)
0600        IF &JDAY LE &TEST, THEN DO
0610                            SET &MONTH = &LOOP + 1
0620                            SET &SWCH = 1
0630                          ENDX
0640        SET &LOOP = &LOOP + 1
0650      ENDX
0660      /* Add leading zero if month is 1 - 9         */
0670      IF &LENGTH(&MONTH) < 2 +
0680        THEN SET &MONTH = &STR(0&MONTH)
0690      /* Set day of month =                         */
0700      /*    Julian day - last day of previous month  */
0710      IF &LPYR = 0, +
0720        THEN SET &TEST = &SUBSTR(&CNTR:&CNTR+2,&TBL3)
0730        ELSE SET &TEST = &SUBSTR(&CNTR:&CNTR+2,&TBL4)
0740      SET &DAY = &JDAY - &TEST
```

```
0750        /* Add leading zero if day is 1 - 9                  */
0760        IF &LENGTH(&DAY) < 2, +
0770           THEN SET &DAY = &STR(0&DAY)
0780        /* Set DATEX to string                               */
0790        /*      Gregorian date mm/dd/yy                      */
0800        SET &DATEX = +
0810          &STR(&STR(&MONTH)&STR(/)&STR(&DAY)&STR(/)&YEAR)
0820        /* Branch to OTHR                                    */
0830        /*      to compute Names, Cmpday, Relday             */
0840        GOTO OTHR
0850        /***************************************************/
0860        /* GREG ---                                          */
0870        /*      Convert input Gregorian to Julian date       */
0880        /*                                                   */
0890        /*      Set Month, Day, Year,                        */
0900        /*          Julian Day, Leap Year                    */
0910        /*                                                   */
0920 GREG:  SET &YEAR = &SUBSTR(7:8,&STR(&DATE)
0930        SET &MONTH = &SUBSTR(1:2,&DATEX)
0940        SET &DAY = &SUBSTR(4:5,&DATEX)
0950        SET &LPYR = &SUBSTR(&YEAR-74,&TBL5)
0960        /* Perform loop to compute Julian day by             */
0970        /*      adding days in MONTBL while relative         */
0980        /*      position (LOOP) is before current month      */
0990        /* If January, loop is not executed because          */
1000        /*      LOOP is not < MONTH                           */
1010        IF &LPYR = 0, +
1020           THEN SET &MONTBL = +
1030                           &STR(3128313031303131303313031)
1040           ELSE SET &MONTBL = +
1050                           &STR(3129313031303131303313031)
1060        SET &JDAY = &DAY
1070        SET &LOOP = 1
1080        DO WHILE &LOOP < &MONTH
1090           SET &CALDAY = &SUBSTR+
1100           (((&LOOP-1)*2)+1:((&LOOP-1)*2)+2,&MONTBL)
1110           SET &JDAY = &JDAY + &CALDAY
1120           SET &LOOP = &LOOP + 1
1130        ENDX
```

```
1140        /* Add 1st leading zero if Julian day is 1-99   */
1150        IF &LENGTH(&STR(&JDAY)) < 3, THEN +
1160           SET &JDAY = &STR(0&JDAY)
1170        /* Add 2nd leading zero if Julian day is 1-9    */
1180        IF &LENGTH(&STR(&JDAY)) < 3, THEN +
1190           SET &JDAY = &STR(0&JDAY)
1200        /* Branch to OTHR                               */
1210        /*     to compute Names, Cmpday, Relday         */
1220        GOTO OTHER
1230        /***********************************************/
1240        /* OTHR ---                                     */
1250        /*    Calculate the Computation Day and Relative */
1260        /*    Day of the Week; Set Name of Month and Day */
1270        /*                                              */
1280        /* Calculate Computation Day                    */
1290 OTHR: SET &CMPDAY = &JDAY
1300        SET &LOOP = 1
1310        DO WHILE &LOOP < (&YEAR - 1974)
1320           SET &CMPDAY = &CMPDAY + 365
1330           IF &SUBSTR(&LOOP,&TBL5) = 1, THEN +
1340                              SET &CMPDAY = &CMPDAY + 1
1350           SET &LOOP = &LOOP + 1
1360        ENDX
1370        /* Set Relative day of the week 1-7             */
1380        /* CMPDAY / 7 is truncated to a whole number    */
1390        /* If answer multiplied by 7                    */
1400        /*    result is = or < original CMPDAY          */
1410        SET &RELDAY = (&CMPDAY - ((&CMPDAY / 7) * 7)) + 3
1420        IF &RELDAY > 7, THEN SET &RELDAY = &RELDAY - 7
1430        /* Set Name of the Month                        */
1440        SET &MONTHN = &SUBSTR+
1450           (((&MONTH-1)*3)+1:((&MONTH-1)*3)+3,&TBL6)
1460        /* Set Name of the Day                          */
1470        SET &DAYN = &SUBSTR+
1480           (((&RELDAY-1)*3)+1:((&RELDAY-1)*3)+3,&TBL7)
1490        /* Set Leap Year to YES or NO                   */
1500        IF &LPYR = 0, THEN SET &LEAPYR = &STR(NO)
1510                     ELSE SET &LEAPYR = &STR(YES)
1520        /***********************************************/
```

```
1530    /* FINI ---                                    */
1540    /*      Exit "DATECALC"                        */
1550    /*      Return to main "DATEPRNT"              */
1560    /*                                             */
1570 FINI: EXIT
```

11

CLIST Error Codes

When a CLIST is first initiated, or during its execution, an error condition may be detected by the system. If an error occurs, an error code will be issued. The table below lists the error codes, the applicable CLIST statement or variable (blank for general errors or for those that occur in various operations), and a description of the error condition.

Error Codes	CLIST Element	Error Condition
016		Insufficient system memory
300		Attempt to modify a system variable
304	EXIT	Invalid operand on statement
308	EXIT	Code specified but no value given
312	GLOBAL	Internal error in processing variable
316	TERMIN	Delimiter with more than 256 characters
324	GETFILE	Error in reading file
328	TERMIN	More than 64 delimiters specified

Error Codes	*CLIST Element*	*Error Condition*
332		Invalid syntax for file name (ddname)
336	OPENFILE	File is already open
340	OPENFILE	Invalid mode type for open
344	OPENFILE	Undefined open mode type
348	OPENFILE	Specified file could not be opened
352	GETFILE	File not currently open
356	GETFILE	File closed by system in another operation
360	PUTFILE	File not currently open
364	PUTFILE	File closed by system in another operation
368	PUTFILE	File not opened by OPENFILE
368	CLOSFILE	File not opened by OPENFILE
372	PUTFILE	Issued before GETFILE on update file
376	OPENFILE	Unable to open directory of VB format PDS
380	PUTFILE	Attempted I/O on record with LRECL > 32767
400	GETFILE	End of file (last record already read)
404	PUTFILE	Attempt to write to file opened for input
408	PUTFILE	Attempt to read from file opened as output
412	PUTFILE	Attempt to update file after end of file
416	PUTFILE	Attempt to update empty file

Error Codes	CLIST Element	Error Condition
500	DO	Non-numeric TO value in DO statement
502	DO	Non-numeric FROM value in DO statement
504	DO	Non-numeric BY value in DO statement
508	SYSCALL	Attempted call to undefined subprocedure
512	RETURN	Statement contains undefined keyword
528	PROC	Invalid positional definition on PROC
532	PROC	Invalid characters in PROC statement
536	PROC	Name of symbolic parameter too long
540	PROC	Too many positional values received
544	PROC	No parameters defined on PROC statement
548	PROC	Duplicate parameter names on statement
552	PROC	Keyword parameter with invalid value
556	PROC	Default keyword value without ending quote
560	PROC	Parse error while processing statement
572	SYSREF	Variable not passed as a parameter
576	SYSREF	SYSREF variable not defined on PROC

Error Codes	CLIST Element	Error Condition
580	ERROR	ERROR found in subprocedure ERROR routine
580	ERROR	ERROR found in subprocedure ATTN routine
584	ATTN	ATTN found in subprocedure ERROR routine
584	ATTN	ATTN found in subprocedure ATTN routine
708	&SYSINDEX	&SYSINDEX expression invalid
712	&SYSINDEX	&SYSINDEX start parameter invalid
716	&SYSNSUB	&SYSNSUB parameter not 0 to 99
720	&SYSNSUB	&SYSNSUB parameter missing
724	&SYSNSUB	&SYSNSUB parameter with built-in function
800		Data found where operator was expected
804		Operator found where data was expected
808	SET	Comparison operator in statement
816		Operator found at end of statement
820		Operators out of order
824		More than 1 exclusive operator
828		More than 1 exclusive comparison operator
832		Value $< -2,147,483,684$ or $> +2,147,483,684$
840		Insufficient number of operands

Error Codes	CLIST Element	Error Condition
844		No valid operators
848		Load character data from numeric value
852		Addition on character data
856		Subtraction on character data
860		Multiplication on character data
864		Division on character data or by zero
868		Prefix found on character data
872		Numeric value too large
900		Single ampersand found
908		Error occurred in ATTN or ERROR DO group
912	&SUBSTR	Substring range not valid
916	&SUBSTR	Value for substring range not numeric
920	&SUBSTR	Value for substring range zero or negative
924	&SUBSTR	Substring syntax not valid
932	&SUBSTR	Value for substring range beyond string
936		Missing operand for built-in function
940		Invalid symbolic variable
944		Label used as a symbolic variable
948	GOTO	Invalid syntax for specified label
952	GOTO	Specified label not in procedure
956	GOTO	Statement does not identify a label

Error Codes	CLIST Element	Error Condition
960	&SYSSCAN	&SYSSCAN variable set to invalid value
964	&LASTCC	&LASTCC variable set to invalid value
968	DATA ...	DATA PROMPT ... ENDDATA but no prompt occurred
972	TERMIN	Statement cannot be executed in batch job
976	READ	Statement cannot be executed in batch job
980		Maximum statement length of 32756 exceeded
999		Internal command procedure error

Exercise Solutions

A.1 SOLUTIONS TO CHAPTER 5 EXERCISES

1. Which of the following statements about CLISTs are false? If not true, why not? What is the correct answer?

False   CLISTs must include one or more CLIST statements and at least one TSO command or subcommand.

It may include any combination of CLIST statements, as well as TSO commands and subcommands. There is no requirement that it must include a CLIST statement, a TSO command or a TSO subcommand so long as it contains at least one of these.

True   The CLIST must be a sequential dataset or member of a partitioned dataset and must be line-numbered.

A CLIST is stored as a sequential dataset or a member in a partitioned dataset. CLISTS must be in line-numbered datasets to be executable by the CLIST interpreter. Names for CLIST statements must be in upper case.

False   A CLIST with a non-standard dataset name may be invoked either by explicit or implicit execution, but not by extended implicit execution.

CLISTs whose dataset names do not end with the standard IBM type "CLIST" can be initiated only by explicit execution. Also, the dataset name in the EXEC command must be fully qualified.

True   A CLIST may consist of only TSO subcommands.

A CLIST may contain only CLIST statements, only TSO commands or only TSO subcommands as well as any valid combination of them. An example is a CLIST that contains only EDIT subcommands and that is executed only when editing a dataset.

False   The default values assigned to the positional and keyword parameters are null values.

Positional parameters have no default value, and the user must enter their values when the CLIST is initiated. Keyword parameters may be given default values on a PROC statement, although the default may be a null value.

2. Each CLIST statement below contains one or more structure and syntax errors. Correct all of the errors. Do not be concerned with any aspect of the statement except for its structure and syntax. Assume that all lines below are in the same CLIST but that this is only a partial list. The PROC statements in line 110 and line 175 define positional and keyword parameters, and values will be specified by a user when the CLIST is initiated. There are 20 errors.

```
040 SET &A = (&B+XYZ) ; GOTO LABELA
```

— The line may have only one statement or only one TSO command or subcommand.
— A semicolon cannot serve as a delimiter.

— Since XYZ is not prefixed with an ampersand, it must be a character string. A character string in an arithmetic computation results in an error condition.

`110 LABELA: PROC 2 VAR1 VAR2(ABC) VAR3(XYZ) VAR4`

— PROC statements that define CLIST initiation parameters must be the first line.
— PROC statements that define CLIST initiation parameters do not have a label.
— The number of positional parameters is coded as two although there is only one. VAR2 has a default value ABC and it must therefore be a keyword parameter.

`150 LABELB. WRITE ENTER YOUR NAME`

— A label must be ended with a colon (:).

`175 PROC 0 &KYWD1() &KYWD2()`

— A PROC statement must be the first line.
— There can be only one PROC statement.
— Variable names on the PROC statement are not prefixed with an ampersand.

`210 IF A EQ &B`

— An IF statement must have a THEN operand and there is no + or − continuation to the next line.

`THEN GOTO 240`

— There is no line number for the statement.
— GOTO statements must refer to a label. They must not specify a line number.

```
250 /* This is a Date routine
```

- There is no closing delimiter (*/).

```
240 SET&DATASET =&DSN.DATA
```

- Line numbers must be in ascending order.
- There must be a space after SET.
- The period after &DSN delimits this variable name. If, for example, the value of &DSN is TEST, the variable &DATASET will be assigned the value TESTDATA when the single period is coded. Therefore, two periods are required, as in the statement SET &DATASET=&DSN..DATA, to result in the dataset name TEST.DATA.

```
275 SET &DATE &MONTH&DAY&1991
```

- SET must include an EQ or = operator.
- Variable names must begin with a letter.

```
290 IF &X = &B, THEN GOTO LABEL5:
```

- The name of the label for the object of GOTO must not be closed by a colon.

A.2   SOLUTIONS TO CHAPTER 8 EXERCISES

1. Match the types of variables listed below with the one or more statements that describe them. Some statements will describe more than one type of variable.

   a. Positional parameter   **e.** Dataset input/output
   b. Keyword parameter   **f.** Terminal input
   c. System-defined   **g.** User-defined
   d. Built-in function   **h.** Global

   a b _____   Defined in a PROC statement

   d _____   Value is determined by evaluating an associated expression

   a b e f g h   Defined by the CLIST writer

   a b c f _____ Receives data from an end user

   d _____   Determines whether a variable is alphanumeric or numeric

   e _____   Contains the contents of one dataset record

   a b h _____   Passes values to nested CLISTs

   c _____   May not be modified in the CLIST (13 system variables can be modified)

   a h _____   Must be defined and read in positional order

   b _____   May be assigned a default value

   a b _____   Values are set initially by a terminal user when the CLIST is initiated

   e _____   Variable name must be identical to the name specified in a TSO command

   c d _____   Automatically available in all levels of nested CLISTs

   g _____   May be initially defined in different kinds of CLIST statements

2. Determine the results of evaluating each of the following expressions. The values of the variables are:

&A = ABC   &B = 120   &C = A2C   &D = 10
&E = e   &F =   &G = 1   &H = 2

Also, assume the current system date is July 4, 1992, the time is 3:30:45 PM and the variable &DATE is equal to the system variable &SYSDATE.

&SYSDATE	07/04/92
&SYSTIME	15:30:45
&DATATYPE(&C)	CHAR
&DATATYPE(&DATE)	NUM
&DATATYPE(&STR(&DATE))	CHAR
&SYSCAPS(&A&E)	ABCE
&SYSLC(&A&STR(&SYSSTIME))	abc15:30
&EVAL(125/(&D/&H))	25
&EVAL((&B+&C+&D)/5)	Error
&LENGTH(&F)	0
&LENGTH(&SUBSTR(&G,&A))	1
&SUBSTR(&G:(&D/&H),&STR(&DATE))	07/04
&SUBSTR(&G:(&D/&H),&DATE)	.0190
&SYSINDEX(C,&A)	3
&SYSINDEX(A,&C,&H)	0
&B + &D / &H	125
(&B + &D) / &H	65
((&G ** &H) - 1)	0

3. Evaluate each of the IF statements below and determine if the condition is true or false. The variables are set to the following values.

&A = ABC   &B = 120   &C = A2C   &D = 10
&E = e   &F =   &G = 1   &H = 2

Also, assume that the current system date is July 4, 1992 and the current time is 3:30 PM.

`IF &A LE &C`	True
`IF &A EQ &C`	False
`IF &B NE (&B * &G)`	False
`IF &G = &LENGTH(&E)`	True
`IF &H GT &LENGTH(&B / &D)`	False
`IF &H < &SUBSTR(4:&D/&H,&STR(&SYSDATE))`	True
`IF &DATATYPE(&E) EQ NUM OR +` `   &LENGTH(&D) EQ &H`	True
`IF &LENGTH(&C) GT &H AND +` `   &D LT &H`	False

A.3 SOLUTIONS TO CHAPTER 9 EXERCISES

1. Write the one or more CLIST statements needed for each of the requirements below.

   a. Code an EXEC command to execute a CLIST named DOIT. A PROC statement that defines one positional parameter named P1 and two keyword parameters named K1 and K2 is required. The keyword variable K1 has a default value of "XYZ" and K2 has a null default value. The CLIST user will specify "10" as a value for P1, will override the default value for K1 with the new value "ABC", and will issue a value of "DEF" for K2.

   ```
   EXEC DOIT 10 K1(ABC) K2(DEF)
   ```

   ```
   PROC 1 P1 K1(XYZ) K2()
   ```

   b. Code a CONTROL statement that will list all executable statements as they are executed, that will display all system messages, that can prevent the CLIST from being flushed if an error condition occurs, and that defines an alternative character string for END.

   ```
   CONTROL SYMLIST MSG NOFLUSH END(ENDX)
   ```

   c. Code a WRITE statement that displays only the current month and day.

   ```
   WRITE &SUBSTR(1:5,&STR(&SYSDATE))
   ```

   d. Code a SET statement that will set the variable &YEAR to the current year in the system date.

   ```
   SET &YEAR EQ &SUBSTR(7:8,&STR(&SYSDATE))
   ```

   e. Code an IF statement using the system variable &SYSDSN to determine if a dataset named "userid.ABC.DATA" is available (value "OK"). If it is, execute the LISTDSI statement to determine the dataset characteristics.

```
IF &SYSDSN('userid.ABC.DATA') = OK, +
```

```
   THEN LISTDSI 'userid.ABC.DATA'
```

f. Code the required SET and GOTO statements to branch to LAB5. The GOTO statement refers to a label name "LAB" with the suffix "&N".

```
SET &N EQ 5
```

```
GOTO LAB&N
```

g. Code an IF–THEN–ELSE statement that tests if a value is numeric. If it is, multiply it by 10, and if it is not, branch to a statement labeled "ERROR". The variable to be tested is named "&TEST".

```
IF &DATATYPE(&TEST) = NUM, +
```

```
       THEN SET &TEST = &TEST * 10
```

```
          ELSE GOTO ERROR
```

h. Execute a compound conditional DO group that examines each position in a character string named &CHAR either until a currency sign ($) is found or until the entire string is examined and no currency sign is found. The search will start with the LAST position and continues backwards to the first position. The variable name of the string is &CHAR and the variable to control the DO loop is named &CNTR.

```
DO &CNTR = &LENGTH(&CHAR) TO 1 BY -1
```

```
   UNTIL &SUBSTR(&CNTR,&CHAR) = &STR($)
```

i. Code a SELECT statement to branch to LABEL1 if the sum of &A and &B is less than 10, to LABEL2 if it is less than 50, or to LABEL3 it is 50 or more.

```
SELECT
```

```
   WHEN ((&A+&B) < 10) GOTO LABEL1
```

```
   WHEN ((&A+&B) < 50) GOTO LABEL2
```

```
   WHEN ((&A+&B) > 49) GOTO LABEL3
```

2. Create a variable named &ALPH and assign as its value all 26 letters of the alphabet. Then perform a DO group that writes the alphabet to the terminal on two separate lines of 13 letters each.

   Only one WRITE statement may be used in the procedure and it is included in the DO group. Use variable names &CTR1 for the number of times the DO group is executed (twice), and &CTR2 and &CTR3 for substring selection.

   Hint: *Set &CTR2 to 1 and &CTR3 to 13 for the first loop of the DO group, and then increment both counters for the second execution of the DO group.*

```
SET &ALPH EQ &STR(ABCDEFGHIJKLMNOPQRSTUVWXYZ)
SET &CTR1 EQ 1
SET &CTR2 EQ 1
SET &CTR3 EQ 13
DO WHILE &CTR1 LT 3
        WRITE &SUBSTR(&CTR2:&CTR3,&ALPH)
        SET &CTR1 EQ &CTR1 + 1
        SET &CTR2 EQ &CTR2 + 13
        SET &CTR3 EQ &CTR3 + 13
    END
```

3. As three separate operations, request the first name, the middle initial and the last name from the terminal user. Add a period after his or her middle initial when the user has omitted it. Then, create a single character string that consists of the first name, middle initial and last name, including proper spacing.

   Use variable names of &FN for the first name, &MI for the middle initial and &LN for the last name. Use a variable name of &FULL for the user's full name.

```
WRITE ENTER YOUR LAST NAME

READ &LN

WRITE ENTER YOUR FIRST NAME

READ &FN

WRITE ENTER YOUR MIDDLE INITIAL

READ &MI

IF &SUBSTR(&LENGTH(&MI),&MI) NE &STR(.) +

     THEN SET &MI EQ &STR(&MI&STR(.))

SET &NAME EQ &STR(&FN&STR( )&MI&STR( )&LN)
```

4. An online dataset is not numbered. In a DO WHILE group, read each record, insert a line number to prefix the data, and write the altered record to a new dataset. However, each input record is to be displayed on the terminal to enable the user to respond with "Y" when the record is to be kept. Therefore, the user can elect to retain or drop records for the output. When the user decides to keep an input record, it is first prefixed with a line number and then written to the output dataset. If the user decides to drop the record, it is simply ignored and the DO group returns to read the next input record.

The first output record is numbered 100 and the number of each successive record is incremented by 100. After all input records are processed, the count of output records is displayed for the user.

Assume that the input and output datasets were allocated previously using the file names OLDFILE for the input and NEWFILE for the output. However, remember that you must first open the files and close them when done.

The variable names are &CNTR to count the output records, &NUMB for the incremental value to number each record, and &LAST to save the return code from each GETFILE. Be sure to test for end-of-file when &LASTCC will be 400, and branch out of the DO group after the last record is read.

```
BEGIN: OPENFILE OLDFILE INPUT
       OPENFILE NEWFILE OUTPUT
       SET &LAST EQ 0
       SET &CNTR EQ 0
       SET &NUMB EQ 100
LOOPS: DO WHILE &LAST EQ 0
          GETFILE OLDFILE
          SET &LAST EQ &LASTCC
          IF &LAST GT 0, THEN GOTO CLOSE
          WRITE &OLDFILE
          WRITE ENTER Y TO WRITE TO NEW FILE
          READ &ANSW
          IF &ANSW EQ Y, THEN DO
                SET &NEWFILE EQ &NUMB&OLDFILE
                PUTFILE NEWFILE
                SET &CNTR EQ &CNTR + 1
                SET &NUMB EQ &NUMB + 100
             END
          END
CLOSE: CLOSFILE OLDFILE
       CLOSFILE NEWFILE
       WRITE &NUMB RECORDS WRITTEN TO NEW FILE
```

Index